SOCIAL SCIENCE AND INDIAN SOCIETY

RANCHI ANTHROPOLOGY SERIES—8

RANCHI ANTHROPOLOGY SERIES

No. 1 : Process, Performance and Pilgrimage : A Study in Comparative Symbology—**Victor Turner**, 1979, Rs. 50 $ 10

No. 2 : Development of Researches in Anthropology in India : Bihar: A Case Study—**L.P. Vidyarthi** and **V.S. Upadhyay** (Eds.), 1981, Rs. 65 $ 13

No. 3 : Nature-Man-Spirit Complex in tribal India—**R.S. Mann** and **Vijoy S. Sahay** (Eds.), 1981, Rs. 70 $ 14

No. 4 : Microevolution—**B.M. Das**, 1981, Rs. 60 $ 12

No. 5 : Tribal Festivals of Bihar : A Functional Analysis —**Ajit K. Singh**, 1982, Rs. 70 $ 14

No. 6 : The Spectrum of the Sacred : Essays on Religious Traditions of India—**B.N. Saraswati**, 1984, Rs. 100 $ 20

No. 7 : Folklore: The Pulse of the People—**Mazharul Islam**, 1985, Rs. 180 $ 36

No. 8 : Social Science and Indian Society : A Civilisational Perspective—**Baidya Nath Varma**, 1985, Rs. 80 $ 16

No. 9 : Museums, The Public and Anthropology—**Michael M. Ames** (*in press*)

RANCHI ANTHROPOLOGY SERIES—8

Gen. Editor : L. P. VIDYARTHI

Social Science and Indian Society

A Civilisational Perspective

BAIDYA NATH VARMA

The City University of New York

CONCEPT PUBLISHING COMPANY, NEW DELHI

First Published 1985

Published by

Naurang Rai
Concept Publishing Company
H-13, Bali Nagar
NEW DELHI-110015 (India)

Printed in India by

Aay Kay Prints
at Mohan Printing Corporation
Padam Nagar
DELHI-110007

GENERAL EDITOR'S INTRODUCTION

THE Department of Anthropology of Ranchi University has celebrated its Silver Jubilee in 1978. Again, it received the recognition of being the only U.G.C. Centre of Special Assistance in Anthropology in the country almost in the same year. During the tenure of my Presidentship of the International Union of Anthropological and Ethnological Sciences (1973-78) as well as the Xth ICAES (1978), the Department was also called upon to perform several academic and professional roles involving in at the international level.

With this background, we ventured to launch a new series of publications entitled "Ranchi Anthropology Series" in the year 1980. This series is designed to provide a short but scholarly treatment of key problem-areas in anthropology. Under this series, in addition to lectures delivered at Ranchi by visiting scholars of national and international repute, we have also been publishing the theoretically-oriented research work of local scholars as well as proceedings of national and international level seminars and symposia.

This volume on Social Science and Indian Society : A Civilisational Perspective has grown out of the lectures delivered by Professor Baidya Nath Varma as Visiting Professor at Ranchi University. Professor Varma received his Ph.D. in Sociology from Columbia University, where he studied theory with Robert K. Merton and methodology with Paul F. Hazarsfeld. He was a consultant to anthropologist Conrad M. Arensburg in his project on India. He was invited by the Anthropology Section of the New York Academy of Sciences to present a paper on methodology under the chairmanship of Margaret Mead. His Paper was published as *A Memoir* by the Academy. As Professor Varma says, "I may be a sociologist but anthropologists are my best friends".

Professor Varma has challenged the social scientist in this book to take up the cause of creative research in helping India solve some of its knotty problems. He has also urged the social leaders to consult social scientists on issues where the competence of the latter is a proven fact. Professor Varma has conducted research on modernisation for the last twenty years in the United States and India. His research trips have taken him to England, Spain, Egypt and Japan among other countries on the four continents. His model of modernisation was presented in his book, *The Sociology and Politics of Development : A Theoretical Study,* which was published in the International Library of Sociology series in London in 1980.

Professor Varma has refuted the scholars who have projected an image of Hinduism as being not conductive to development. He has provided a critique of the voluminous philosophical literature in the field by also drawing widely on anthropological data. His own view of the modernisation of India is portrayed in a succint but lucid form, where he projects a clear picture of India's future, provided the recent trends continue. He also delineatus alternative scenarios for india if the situation happens to change radically as described by him. Professor Varma never forgets that he is primarily a theorist ("an allowed theorist" as he call himself) and so his articles are full of hypotheses about the development of society, whether it concerns family, religion, acculturation, or what have you. He says that the civilisational perspective has been neglected by sociologists in the recent past and this has skewed their findings. He brings to the analysis of the Indian immigrants in the United States the civilisational framework of India which throws new light on the assimilation of the Asian Indians in the United States. There is much food for thought for the social scientist in this short volume and I recommend it highly to the scholars and even the general readers.

Director, U.G.C. Centre of Special Assistance in Anthropology and University Professor and Head, Department of Anthropology, Ranchi University, Ranchi

L.P. VIDYARTHI

28 August 1985

INTRODUCTION

SOCIAL Science has provided a perspective on Indian society; however, it is not clear how far the civilisational point of view has been imbued in it. The present series of articles is meant to throw light on this issue.

Social Science is relatively new in the evolution of sciences. Science deals with reality and this reality has been explored by the seers of India from time immemorial. The Vedas, the most sacred books of the Hindus, were meant to explore knowledge. The word 'Veda' is a derivation of the verb 'vid', i.e., *to know*. In the Isha Upanishad, the first of the Upanishads, which were learnt by students "sitting down" near the holy teacher, there is the injunction:

> The threshold of reality is veiled by golden light.
> Reveal it, O Lord, for my *dharma* is to know the truth.

Scholars of Indian civilisation have pursued the path of knowledge in a multifarious way, the most germane for our purposes being the Upa Vedas and the Vedangas. The Upa Vedas are four in number: Ayurveda, the science of life (medicine); Dhanurveda, the science of archery (weapons); Gandharva Veda the science of music and dance (artistic creation); and Arthashastra, the science of politics (administration, commerce, law and order). The Vedangas among others consist of the well-known books of grammar and phonetics written by Panini; and books on etymology, prosody as well as the famous, Jyotish Shastra, the science of astronomy and astrology.

The concept of zero (shunya) evolved in India and so did the numerals which are known in the West as the Arabic numeral system, because the Arabs borrowed it from India. Aryabhata, an Indian astronomer, had said that the earth rotated on its axis around the sun even before this phenomenon was discovered in the West. Thus the tradition of seeking knowledge of worldly phenomena, which today is covered by the terms natural sciences, life sciences and social sciences is quite ancient in the life of the Hindus and later on of others who have inhabited the land called Bharatvarsa or India.

It is not our intention to downgrade here the knowledge provided by present day social science about Indian society. However, social science, as I have shown elsewhere,[1] is impregnated with values and as such the generalisations of many Western social scientists about Indian society are increasingly being questioned today. It is to throw light on some of these issues that the present set of papers were prepared. India is going through modernisation today and the ramifications of the modernisation process have to be fathomed.

The first article in this book is a challenge to the social scientist to incorporate the cultural tradition (involving civilisational values) in his repertoire and then proceed in his scientific analysis of the issue under investigation. Without it, the study will remain barren at best or ethnocentric (westernised) at worst. The second article examines the interrelations of religion and development in India. Many myths about Hinduism standing in the way of India's progress are exploded here. The next article gives a global picture of India's modernisation at the current juncture in its history and economy. I have stated the grounds of my commitment to theory (*siddhanta*) in these articles. In order to test some of my ideas (including hypotheses), I have analysed in the next two articles the situation of the

1. Baidya Nath Varma, *The Sociology and Politics of Development : A Theoretical Study*, London : Routledge and Kegan Paul, 1980.

Indians who have migrated to the United States in this century. How far the civilisational values of the Indians help or hinder their assimilation in the country they have chosen to settle in is the main burden of these articles. I believe that the hypotheses presented by me specially about the health and well-being of the Indian family, the socialisation of the young and the care of the old will hold for all Indians in over sixty countries of the world to which they have migrated. In the end, it is the civilisational values which sustain man wherever he is located.

I am grateful to Professor Lalita Prasad Vidyarthi for providing me the opportunity to test my ideas before a learned audience at Ranchi University.

New Delhi
July 1985

BAIDYA NATH VARMA

CONTENTS

THE MEETING OF TWO CULTURES: SOCIAL SCIENCE AND THE CULTURAL TRADITION OF INDIA

1

The Meeting of Two Cultures : Social Science and the Cultural Tradition of India

IT may sound strange to suggest that social science has a culture of its own. However, if the word culture is used in the sense of created traditions and accumulated heritage, there is no difficulty in using this word for the social scientific enterprise in which the intellectuals have been engaged for at least a couple of centuries. The cumulative body of knowledge created through the efforts of social scientists, the tools and the equipments they use and the social organisation of their work comprise a cohesive system, which no doubt qualifies to match the best of cultures. Science as a growing body of knowledge and social science as a part of that mainstream are together vying for an important place in the totality of cultures that are represented on the modern world stage.

The cultural tradition of India is a mammoth edifice. In its civilisational contours, it has a recognisable shape and quality of its own. Some people identify its rubrics as being composed of a divinely ordained hierarchical order ; limited potentialities of the individual with limitless scope for his advancement along fixed lines ; a structural constraint, as exhibited in the *varna* order of the Hindus and self-subsisting existences of Muslims, Christians, Parsees, tribals and others, each no doubt linked to the other in certain spheres of activities and yet retaining an autonomy for most purposes of social intercourse ; and finally an ingrained faith in traditonalism often leading to a glorification of the past. Thus, belief in divinity, hierarchy, ordained limitations and potentialities of individuals, compartmentalisation of social existences of groups, and positive valuation of the past seem to be the hallmarks of Indian culture. Others emphasise the remarkable secularisation of even aspects of the divine (*e.g.*, in *Krishna Lila*), the ingrained respect for the individual's personality in spite of the hierarchical order, the growth potentials of each member of the society (as stated in the epigram *Soham*), the linkages of the groups in the social order of rural India (*e.g.*, in the concept of "my village" and also what the sociologists call the *jajmani* system), and the transvaluation of the past for meeting the current and future needs of the Indian body social.

It is difficult to choose between these interpretations as genuinely applying to contemporary India. They both seem on the surface to be right depending on which side of the coin one is looking at. It is no doubt true that the former view emphasises stability and being and believes this to be the key to Indian culture, the latter view holds up the notion of change and becoming as forming the essential basis of the evolution of Indian culture. Both views may perhaps be right in the light of their own perspectives because Indian culture represents an accretion along certain broad themes as well as a conglomeration of various streams of socio-cultural phenomena. However, I wish to point out that an excessive justification of the past may lead to schizophrenic tendencies just as an unnecessary rejection of the ancient landmarks of culture may ensue in wide scale anomia.

Modern India faces a great acceleration in its cultural tempo. The cherished values of the family (the joint family system), the community (the caste system), the polity (the *varna* order and its interconnections with the *non-varna* frameworks) are giving in to the onslaught of the machine age. People's work-a-day life and individual as well as group pursuits are changing so rapidly that it is difficult to discern any direction in them at the moment. The tools of social science no doubt will be applied for purposes of analysis of the present and prognosis of the future but this takes time. Indian social scientists are still not quite sure of themselves.

The Indian masses are on the move, Indian polity is afloat. Neither is willing to wait. Whether our social scientists come to the aid or not, people will act, decisions will be made. I believe it is the responsibility of the social scientists *qua* social scientists to provide light on important issues of the day as the scientists bring them into their grips with their specialised research tools. People speak with many voices, the politicians articulate their voice into a few issues of debate, the social scientists must narrow the range still further by their objective analyses of the situation. The people's voice speaks in terms of felt needs, the policy maker's voice speaks in terms of accomplishable felt needs, the social scientist's voice must speak in terms of latent needs of developing society. The protocol of the scientist is always public ; his assumptions, tools, and findings are open to inspection by qualified people at all times. It is the objectivity and the neutrality of the scientist and his search for excellence which have given the culture of science and knowledge a respected place in the court of public opinion in modern times.

I know that science itself is capable of carrying many controversies within its four walls. These controversies may refer to the assumptions of science or to its tools and techniques. They may also refer to the question of priorities in the kinds of research to be undertaken as well as the place of applied research in the development of the culture of science. But in my opinion, faith in science or justification for its existence should not be called into question. Modern world with its global communication and logistic networks, its mounting problems of population growth, and increasing trends of urbanisation and industrialisation cannot afford to live without science. The danger is not that there will be no scientists, but that there may be so much science and its application that individuals will lose autonomy and human dignity. However, there is reason for hope, because the creativity of the human being should be guarantee enough to make science the servant of his works rather than the master of his destiny.

I should also like to put in a word of caution. I believe that no one today needs to be convinced of the value of science. What I am afraid of is a lapse of judgement on the part of scientists. I have seen many a social scientist talk like a politician and many a sociologist talk like a social philanthropist. If we abjure our role of scientist, if we forsake the tools of science for the tools of politics in our scientific enterprise we would have failed in our duty. Posterity will pass harsh judgement on such aberration on the part of social scientists. I am, however, not derogating the role of the scientist in guiding policy decisions.

I hope that the various issues connected with the value of social science for modern life, its development in specific directions, the nourishment it needs and the ends to which it can be put will be frankly and forcefully debated in the coming years, especially since our new Prime Minister, Shri Rajiv Gandhi, has given a valued role to the educationists in the country. There are some intradisciplinary controversies which need to be settled, there are some inter-disciplinary squabbles which need to be straightened out. We want the support of the social leaders for the nourishment of the culture of social science, just as the leaders and citizens of the Indian body polity need our assistance for the solution of some of their knotty problems of existence and growth.

In so far as science is cumulative, knowledge should be made cumulative. It should be used in the service of mankind. In this endeavour, both the scientist and the leaders must join hands. It would not do for the social scientist to live in the ivory tower of his grand theories and dazzling research equipments, just as it would not behoove the leaders of any nation to take a condescending if not spurning attitude toward the culture bearers of social science. Life in the atomic age is too complex and the coming struggle of the human mind and spirit against mechanisation is too imminent to permit us to forget the precariousness of our situation. I earnestly hope that the distinguished leaders of science and society will not only underscore the value of science through their pronouncements and performances but will also provide a meeting ground for the two cultures : the culture of social science and the culture of *bharat bhoomi*—the land and people that constitute India.

HINDUISM AND INDIA'S DEVELOPMENT

2

Hinduism and India's Development

INTRODUCTION

A DISCUSSION of the role of religion in a nation's development has to take into account two important controversies. One concerns the general question whether religious values and precepts have a determining influence on secular action, the other poses the special question whether Max Weber's thesis on the development of capitalism as an unanticipated consequence of the Protestant Ethic (Weber 1950) has any relevance for ordering the problems of the developing nations. Much has been written regarding the barriers which the religions of the East present to the modernisation of their home countries. It has also been suggested that a functional equivalent to the Protestant Ethic has to be created if these nations are to prosper both materially and spiritually. In the great debate on modernisation, economic growth is sometimes considered to be a pro-condition to moral growth.

It would defeat our purpose if we took sides on these issues at the outset. The arguments are much too complex, and the relevant facts are not yet ascertained. As we shall show later, a great deal of research needs to be done on the social structure of modernising nations before either of the controversies can be resolved. However, our examination of the Indian case should help clarify some important problems connected with these issues.

The analysis of the impact of religion on national development needs clarification on three more points. One relates to causation, another to method, and the third to the comparative framework. The causal difficulty in this case refers to the impact of ideas on social practice. Max Weber, as we noted earlier, gave great weight to the importance of religious ideas and ideals in the determination of economic interest. The potency of ideas has been universally claimed as influencing human behaviour, Karl Marx not withstanding. As Sidney Hook has pointed out, "there is a certain social connection between doctrine and practice which is less than logical, more than personal, and other than casual" (Hook 1962:23).

The method used for analysing the interrelations of the values and norms of one institutional sector with those of another needs to be made quite explicit. The way religious values and norms are defined, selected, analysed, and correlated is often only implicit in the analyst's mind. We believe that a clear statement of the methods used in assessing the values and their interrelations would be helpful in the appraisal of the situation.

The comparative framework implies that societies be viewed in some context; for example, in our case it would be the context of the secularisation process. However, secularisation itself has two meanings in the published literature. When a certain society is put on the secular end of the sacred-secular continuum, it may mean either that the major institutions are sufficiently differentiated and compartmentalised so that the religious norms and values have equal standing with, say, the economic; or that, despite the differentiation, religious values although generally neutralised permeate and perhaps guide other secular institutions in the developmental process.[1]

Having taken note of these basic difficulties, we will now consider separately each variant in the equation concerning Hinduism and India's development. Our analysis will be geared to examining religious values and attitudes which facilitate or obstruct India's national development. We will look for both anticipated and unanticipated consequences of religious beliefs, practices, and value systems for other institutional sectors. We will see if functionally relevant traits for socio-economic development are existent in Hinduism. We will also ascertain if "break throughs" in the value systems are possible, which may give fillip to the modernisation process.

THE RELIGIOUS VARIANT

Eighty-five per cent of India's population is Hindu, and their religion is Hinduism. Hinduism is more than a philosophy or religion. It is a way of life. It has been claimed that Buddhism, Jainism and, to some extent, even Sikhism fall within the purview of Hinduism. We will first examine the world-view which Hinduism fosters and then discuss those aspects of Hinduism which may be helpful in understanding the national development of India.

A Controversy

Some authors have taken the diverse strands of Hindu metaphysics, epistemology, and ethics and constructed a *Weltanschauung* for Hindus, which has run into a deep controversy. F. S. C. Northrop, a philosopher of science and comparative religions, claimed that the Eastern perspective including the Indian is dominated by naive realism, aesthetic components (referring to the realm of immediate, direct, even sensory awareness of physical nature and people in an undifferentiated continuum), and concepts by intuition, whereas the Western perspective partakes of radical empiricism in epistemic correlation with logical realism, rational and theoretic components, and knowledge by postulation (which, in whole or part, are concepts by intellection) (Northrop 1946, 1952). Given such a premise, the conclusion drawn by him is irresistible : "A culture which admits only concepts by intuition is automatically prevented from developing science of the Western type beyond the most elementary, inductive, natural history stage" (Northrop 1944 : 212). Some Indian and Chinese philosophers have questioned the judgement of Northrop on this point (Arapura 1953; Hu 1962).

Some have characterised the Eastern religions and philosophies as quietistic, and leading to pacifism ; the Hindu ethic, in their judgement, fosters a negative attitude toward the world of material things. W.H. Workmeister, although realising the practicality of Eastern philosophy, comments :

> The most striking feature of Oriental philosophy, it seems to me, is its concern with the status of man in this world (China) and with man's ultimate goal (India). It is my impression that this interest in man clearly predominates over any interest in Nature or in God. As a result of this man-centered orientation, the philosophies of the East are primarily practical—designed to provide a guide for life, for the attainment of peace of mind. Theoretical considerations, as we find than in the scientifically minded West, play only a secondary part [Workmeister 1962 : 136].

To such controversial statements, Indian philosophers give spirited replies, emphatically stating that science has existed and flourished in India in the past and is making important strides now ; that the early *mimāmsas* of the vedas and the *Bhagavad Gītā* (perhaps the most influnential religious scripture of the Hindus) gives importance to active life ; that the religio-political literature of India sanctions three-fold human values (*trivarga*)—*dharma* (morality), *artha* (wealth), and *kāma* (enjoyment) ; that along with these three temporal or instrumental values there is a fourth value, called *moksa* (release), which is intrinsic and eternal. The primacy of *moksa* over other values as well as *Niṣkāma Karma* ("desireless action") of the *Bhagavad Gitā* no doubt suggests attitudes of other worldliness and asceticism. However, the creative interpreters of Indian scriptures recognise in these values "the inwardness of man, of its [Indian religious thought's] freedom, dignity, sacredness, and importance" (Raju 1962 : 287). As S. Radhakrishnan puts it :

> Knowledge is confined to the world of objects, but the self is comprehended from within. There is objective knowledge as well as subjective comprehension.
>
> Metaphysical thinking which bases itself on experience, holds that Nature is grasped with the concept of necessity and the nature of the self by that of freedom. Without this concept, our understanding of man's nature will be deficient and distorted. [Radhakrishnan 1962 : 259].

As will be apparent from this brief summation of the controversy there is no over-all theoretical framework in terms of which the issues of this debate can be resolved. Our position in this regard is that Hindu *Weltanschauung* as presented by various philosophers is a "constructed system," and the method of selection from the multitudes of scriptures, representativeness of the ideas, and levels of abstractions have not been made clear by the authors.

A Way of Resolving The Controversy

An understanding of religion through metaphysics, epistemology and ethics is an intellectual understanding through logical reasoning. Such a "constructed system" tends to be abstract and general. Since we found that there is not enough agreement on some of the basic questions (for instance, activism vs pacifism ; this worldliness vs other worldliness) which may have relevance for India's developmental goals, it may be useful to look instead to the behavioural dimensions of the religious phenomenon. There the system will tend to be more concrete and specific and any intellectual description of values will be subject to empirical verification.

Hinduism has no fixed creeds, dogmas, doctrines, or rituals ; any selection of these depends on the individual perception of the selector ; and in this the analyst can be as much in dilemma as the culture bearers of such values. However, once the values have been selected by the culture bearer, they will have important consequences for his action.

HINDU COSMOS

Religion has always defined man's relation to fellow man, to nature, and to the supernatural. We will examine some of these questions in the context of the living traditions of Hinduism in India. First, we will consider the nature of the Ultimate ; second, the nature of sacred roles; third, festivals associated with the worship of the holy (and the unholy), fasts, and religious feasts; and, fourth, religious orientations of the Hindus. This procedure will help to identify behaviourally the primary objects of valuation, as well as the value system of India in terms of which individuals interact with each other and shape their collective destiny.

The nature of the ultimate

The Hindus comprehend the Ultimate through the following kinds of concepts :

(a) *The Absolute* or Brahman. He cannot be defined because He is the ground from which qualities emerge, and He is the Supreme Being, into whom all qualities emerge. In the popular version, it is put as follows, "*neti neti kah Veda pukāre*" (When you have exhausted all description of Him, the Vedas say, 'that is not the end, that is not the end,").

(b) *The Trinity of Gods* (*Trivarga*)

Brahmā—the creator
Viṣṇu—the preserver
Śiva—the destroyer or the transformer

The spouse of Brahmā is Sarasvatī, the goddess of learning and arts ; the spouse of Viṣṇu is Lakṣmī, the goddess of wealth, the spouse of Śiva is Pārvatī, one of whose manifestations is Kālī, goddess of destruction. Viṣṇu comes down in various incarnations to protect the world from evil. Nine past incarnations have been identified ; the tenth is still to come.

(c) *The Deities.* These may be classified as follows:[2]

(*i*) *istadevatā*—the deity preferred, chosen, or received from the *guru* (the religous preceptor) by each individual;

(*ii*) *grhadevatā*—the chief deity for the family or the household, installed in the family shrine. He or she may be accompanied by minor deities, whose number can be increased or reduced under certain circumstances. The chief deity may be common to the lineage, or clan;

(*iii*) *kuladevatā*—the chief deity for the lineage, or clan;

(*iv*) *grāmadevatā*—the deity of the village;

(*v*) *sthānadevatā*—the deity for the locality. For him or her, there are special worship days during the year; often there are also festivals and fairs in his or her honour; also he or she can be the object of pilgrimage;

(*vi*) *prāntadevatā*—the deity of the region, having the same associated functions as *sthānadevatā*, but for a larger territory;

(*vii*) *desadevatā*—The deity for the country, having the same functions as *sthānadevatā*;

(*viii*) *rsidevatā*—the deity like personages,, historical or mythical.

The family shrine and the village, local, regional, and national shrines may have satellites of deities along with the chief deity housed together. Most of these deities are believed to grant special kinds of favours to the devotees, such as intellect, wealth, prestige, health, etc. The deities have power to reward, punish and forgive. The attitudes towards them range from those of awe and reverence to love and fear.

The marriageable girls, the betrothed couple, and the newlyweds are all expected to avoid malevolent deities as well as those places inhabited by spirits or ghosts. The men in general, and those women who have been married long, as well as widows, do not have to practice such avoidance. The position of the children is not quite clear on observing such taboos.

There is an overlap between religious, sectarian, cultic, and congregational gatherings in the worship of the gods and the deities.[3]

SACRED ROLES

The following are the sacred roles in Hinduism:

(*i*) family chaplain (*pūrohit*)—he performs the pujā (worship) and other sacred rites for the family;

(*ii*) family lower chaplain (*mahāpātra*)—he presides over parts of the sacred rites associated with death;

(*iii*) the householder or *jajmān* (client) in his sacred role;

(*iv*) family ritual assistant (*purjan*, e.g., barber, potmaker, etc.);

(*v*) reciter (*kathābacak*) of sacred books (especially the *Purānas* and the Epics) before family gatherings and congregations of people;

(*vi*) astrologer (*jyotishi*)—he prepares horoscopes, determines auspicious dates for various sacred and secular functions in the lives of individuals, families, and community at large;

(*vii*) medicine man and *shaman* (*ojhā*, *guni*, etc.);

(*viii*) family preceptor (*kula guru*)—he gives the sacred formula (*mantra*) to the head of the family as well as to other married adults;

(*ix*) sectarian or cultic preceptor—he gives the sacred formula (*mantra*) to individual adults, who become his disciples or followers;

(*x*) learned man (*pandit*), who knows the sacred books and can advise the householder as well as be the source of pride for residents of a community;

(*xi*) learned man residing and teaching in religious school (*gurukul pandit*);

(*xii*) local temple priest (*mandir ke pujari*);

(*xiii*) temple estate owner (*mahanth*);

(*xiv*) priest (*pandā*) of places of pligrimage—some of them claim exclusive ancestral rights to serve their *jajmān* (client) families around the country;

(*xv*) holy man with established congregation (*āśramavāsī munī*, *yogi*);

(*xvi*) wandering holy man (*sādhu, sannyāsi*);

(*xvii*) prestigeous interpreter of the religious scriptures—he is charismatic leader, who often starts a cult, sect or denomination;

(*xviii*) religio-social reformer, such as Mahatma Gandhi, Vinoba Bhave;

(*xix*) itinerant religious entertainer (e.g., *bhāt*);

(*xx*) beggar, who may be considered holy in places of pilgrimage or on public occasion.

The above list of roles suggests the range but does not exhaust the scope of sacred roles available for Hindus in India today. These roles have not been ordered on a heirarchical basis, because the principle of ranking may apply to some and not to others. Some of these roles are reserved for the *brāhman* (priestly) caste members, others are open to all. Some of the roles are considered necessary for the fulfillment of the sacred obligations and falt needs of the family (roles i to viii) ; others assist householder and the community but are not considered essential for the performance of familial duties and obligations (roles ix to xiv) ; and still others exist for serving the sacred needs of the larger society (roles xv to xx).

It may be noted that a preceptor's (*guru*) main function is to start a husband and wife individually or jointly on the spiritual road to release (*mukti* or *moksa*). The temples and pilgrimages, monasteries and congregations, holy men and saints highlight the sacred order of the Hindu tradition outside the family ; their blessings are available to the householder as well as the renunciator of family obligations.

FESTIVALS, FASTS AND RELIGIOUS FEASTS

The celebrations of the Hindus can be divided into two categories, cyclical and non-cyclical.

Cyclical Events

(*i*) *Rites de passage*

birth ; initiation (*curakarna*) for the *dvija* "twice born" castes and *mundana* (shaving of the head), which is also available to the sudra castes if they are following the path of "sanskritisation," *i e.*, the raising of the ritual status of a caste through adopting values of upper caste [Srinivas 1956] ; betrothal ; marriage; relinquishing of religous vows at old age (e.g., *ekādasi udyāpana*, *tulsi yajna*, etc.) ; death ; death anniversaries ; etc. ;

(*ii*) occasion for fast (as on Sundays or Tuesdays) and family worship of deities ;

(*iii*) festival or observance connected with mythological events (e. g., *dasaharā*, *holi*, etc.) ;

(*iv*)group singing (*kīrtan*) with musical instruments in honour of gods and deities—may be daily, weekly or monthly event ;

(*v*) birth anniversery of holy man and saint ;

(*vi*) feeding the poor on civic occasions.

Noncyclical Events

(*i*) celebrations and feasts for the fulfillment of a wish or success, power, health, prosperity of individuals, families, groups, communities or nation (e. g., *pujā*, *kīrtan*, *yajña*) ;

(*ii*) offerings in crisis situations in order to alleviate disease, epidemic, drought, faminc, etc ;

(*iii*) religious conferences (*dharma sabhās*) ;

(*iv*) sacred ways of initiating significant actions by individuals, families, groups, communities, and the nation (e.g., building a house, well, pond, school, factory, embankment, bridge ; planting trees ; starting on a pilgrimage ; taking an examination; joining a new job ; putting on new clothes ; etc.).

In the category of cyclical events, the first two items are connected with individual and familial welfare ; the remaining items refer to functions concerned with the good of the community. In the noncyclical events, the first two items are again connected with rituals and propitiation for personal or familial gain ; the last two are supposed to help the community, sometimes also individuals and families, in their sacred as well as secular spheres of activities. A certain degree of overlap always exists between individual, familial, and community activities of sacred nature.

RELIGIOUS ORIENTATIONS

A Hindu can adopt any one of the following religous orientations :

(*i*) *karma mārga* : the way of action and duties ;

(*il*) *bhakti mārga* : the way of devotion ;

(*iii*) *jñana mārga* : the way of knowledge.

These are equally open to the householder as well as to the recluse, expcept that the first two are more suited to the life of the familiy man and the last one to that of a hermit or monk.

HIGH HINDUISM

Now that we have considered the nature of the Ultimate, the kinds of sacred roles, the types of sacred rites and celebrations, and the religious orientations of the Hindus, it may be helpful to consider the interrelations of what we would like to refer to as High Hinduism and Popular Hinduism.

By High Hinduism, we mean the core of all past scriptural principles and injunctions, and by Popular Hinduism, we mean current forms of sacred beliefs and actions found in the Hindu communities of India at any specific time. We want to note in this connection that our classification is similar to Robert Redfield's distinction between Great Tradition and Little Tradition (Redfield 1955, 1956), except that Mckim Marriott (Mariott 1955) and others who have adopted his terminology have used the pantheon and the rituals to define the Great Tradition, but we think that ethical injunctions and metaphysical conceptions account for High Hinduism better. M.N. Srinivas has used the concepts of all-India Hinduism, peninsular Hinduism, regional

Hinduism, and local Hinduism, which again articulate all these in terms of deities and "sanskritization" of rituals and beliefs (Srinivas 1956). We believe that the empirical versions of the pantheon, sacred roles, festivals (along with fasts and feasts), and religious orientations described by the anthropologists in various community studies should refer to the behavioural level of popular Hinduism rather than the intellectual level of High Hinduism (cf. Mandelbaum 1964: 10).

Scriptures

The principles of High Hinduism are articulated on a philosophical level, and their ethical and moral commitments can be interpreted in the light of the sacred scriptures and commentaries there on. The Vedas, along with the *Brāhmaṇas*, the *Upaniṣads*, the *śrauta* and *grhya sutras*, the *dharma śastras*, the epics (the Mahābhārata and the Rāmāyana), the *Purāṇas* and the *Agamas*, form the scriptural source of most Hindu precepts and practices.

The Vedas are revealed principles of the divine order, the *Brāhmaṇas* are prose commentaries on the Vedas and are the philosophical treatises, the final portion of these being called *Upaniṣads*. All these treatises are called *Sutras* (thread or clue);they are based on *Śrūti* (hearing), and are revealed ritual and customary laws as handed down to posterity by ancient sages. Together these, treatises form the *Śrauta Sutras*. The rest of the sacred treatises constitute *Grhya Sutrâs*; they are based on *Smrti* (tradition). Manusmriti (or the code of Manu) is one of the more well-known of these *Smritis*. The Mahabhārata and the Rāmayāna are two of the well-known books of scriptural history and ethics; the *Bhagavad Gītā* constituting a part of the former eplc. These two epics have been translated in all vernacular languages and often have somewhat differing versions of the stories. They are generally invoked when religious sanctions are sought for secular behaviour, or when role models of the Hindu tradition need to be highlighted. The *Purāṇas* are didactic treatises and provide sectarian enunciation of sacred obligations They are derived from the latter portion (*Araṇyakas*) of the *Brāhmaṇas*. The *Agamas* are books of rituals.

Fundamental Principles

According to an established tradition, primacy is usually given to the Vcdas; otherwise, none of the other sacred texts are supposed to have inherent precedence over the others. This is the principle of *ekavākyatā* (one utterance) which the commentators and digest makers of Hindu scriptures have generally followed.

High Hinduism places emphasis on the following basic concepts:

(*i*) cyclical view of time;

(*ii*) rebirth, or the principle of *karma*;

(*iii*) sacred duties, or the principle of *dharma*;

(*iv*) renunciation: of fruits of action (*niṣkāma karma*): of attachment to kith and kin (*vānaprastha* and *sannyasa* in advanced stages of life; of life itself (*mukti* or *mokṣa*). This is the ascetic strain in Hinduism;

(*v*) non-violence (*ahiṁsā*). It is an important influence of Buddhism and Jainism on Hinduism;

(*vi*) spiritual individualism (*tattwamasi*—that thou art), giving primacy to the principle of perfectability of man.

Varna Order

The *varṇāsrama dharma*, which is supposed to translate the principles of High Hinduism into behavioural standards, divides society into four classes (*i.e.*, *varṇas*; literally "colour") ranked hierarchically. These classes starting from the uppermost one are;

brāhmaṇs (men of knowledge and learning);

kṣatriyas (men of valour);

vaiśyas (men of business and craft);

śudras (men of labour and manual work).

Hinduism prescribes for the first three classes of people known as *dwiga* (twicc born) four stages of life, viz. *brahmacarya* (studentship), *grhasthya* (householdership), *vānaprastha* (forest life) and *sannyāsa* (renunciation of the world and adoption of the life of a wandering monk). In actual practice, the *varna* system has been transformed into the caste system of India, whose features are well known, and the last two stages of the *āsrama* system are observed more in their breach than adherence.

POPULAR HINDUISM

When one examines the range of beliefs and practices of the Hindus, one is struck more by its diversity than by its unity. From the henotheism of the vedas to the monotheism of Sankara's *advaita vedānta* (the monistic philosophy of Sankara), or the atheism of the philospher, Caravaka, or speculative pantheism of the masses, there is no end to the ways in which the Ultimate Principle or the highest sacred object of valuation has been visualised in its various manifestations. The ways of God realisaton and codes of ethical behaviour are similarly ordered into disparate systems fitting the circumstances of various epochs and needs of various types of people. Without any constraint of dogma, Hinduism, like Judaism, has enjoyed supreme intellectual freedom, both in its philosophical and behavioural spheres.

Diversity

The *varṇāsrama dharma* system, as we noted, is the institutional order of the Hindu society. However, traditionally

Hinduism has permitted variations in beliefs and practices, which has given rise to many denominations, sects and cults. These have been constantly incorporated in the mainstream of Popular Hinduism. Thus a great deal of religious freedom exists for individuals, groups and communities within the Hindu fold. There have been no sharp cleavages between the sacred and the secular, because ideally the sacred is supposed to guide the secular in Hindu society. And realistically some of the secular practices have been generally incorporated into the sacred through a revaluation of the received cannons of the sacred books. But in this process, there have been religious conflicts and doctrinal cleavages also in the past leading to major transvaluations (to wit, the rise of Buddhism, Jainism, Vaisnavism, Tantrism, Śaivism, Śaktism, etc.), but in due course newer doctrines have been accepted as integral parts of Hinduism.

Beliefs

The principle of perfectability of man in the pursuit of the Ultimate is an important value for the Hindus. It has however given rise to a condition, whereby individual interpretations have often created conflicting loyalties. Loyalty to the goal of release (*mūkti*) from rebirth; to the societal goals set by the *sanātan dharma* (or traditional religion, which is generally interpreted as the injunctions of the *varṇāsrama dharma*); to the group goals set up individually by the caste, cult, sect, or donomination; to political goals set by the ruling elite may create conditions of *anomie* ; such situations have often existed- in Indian history. It is thus impossible to assert with any degree of confidence what are the true beliefs and value-orientations of Hinduism. Achievement and success, activity and work, moral orientations and humanitarian values, efficiency and practicality, freedom of the individual and conformity with the group, scientific and secular rationality, democracy and dignity of the individual, racism and fanaticism have all been practiced in the past and any set of such divergent principles has received primacy at one period of Indian history or another. The conception of a modern democracy based on economic prosperity, political consensus, and dignity of the individual is not quite an anathema to the Hindu sacred order; it can be made an integral part of its all encompassing view, through a process of transvaluation.

We have noted the difficulty in arriving at any set of values for Hindus which can be called the core values, unless one thinks solely of the values of High Hinduism. In fact, the climate of opinion in the recent past has been such that it has given rise to a kind of universalism. Most values of the Judco-Christian tradition with which India has been in close touch would have their counterparts in Hinduism today. The following remarks of Gerhard Lenski would apply with equal cogency to Hinduism, if we substituted "India" for "the western world" and "Hindu" for "Judiac Christian" in the quotation :

> In the religious tradition of the Western World, various types of religious orientations have competed with one another, each emphasising a different facet of the Judiac-Christian heritage. Among the more prominent are mysticism, devotionalism, asceticism, ceremonialism, doctrinal orthodoxy, millenialism, and ethicalism. Sometimes individuals emphasise one orientation to the almost total exclusion of the others; sometimes several orientations are cultivated simultaneously. Over the years the relative importance of these orientations has shifted many times as one, then another, gained the ascendancy; but all survive to the present day (Lenski 1963:24).

Behavioural Standards

We will examine briefly some concrete evidence of religious behaviour gleaned from current social-anthropological literature. Belief in God, rebirth, sin (*pāp*), release (*mukti*), renunciation, and ascribed caste differences has been found to be common in the villages. (Opler 1950:315; Harper 1964). Some of these values as we noted earlier, are also associated with High Hinduism. However, there is less consistency from caste to caste with regard to the metaphysical conceptions involved in them (Lewis 1965 [1958] : 249-259). On the other hand, the impact of the humanistic and scientific ideals of the West on Indian elite has filtered to the masses and has sometimes radically changed their perspectives. The rural elite today are often found to be Westernising their way of life, whereas some lower castes are either Westernising or Sanskritising their ideals and behaviour (Gough 1955:49; Cohn 1955). The changes observed in both directions are significant and their importance cannot be minimised. Pauline Mahar reports on the changing religious practices of an untouchable caste in an Indian village :

> Under the influence of Arya Samaj (a socio-religious movement) reforms, the social unit of advancement was the caste brotherhood (*birādari*) as a whole; with secular educational opportunities, the unit of advancement seems to have become the individual more than the group. The religious beliefs and practices associated with the varying modes of advancement have also tended to change the unit of worship from group and household to role units based upon age, sex and education (Mahar 1960:280).

The reference in the last sentence is to the fact that young men of the caste are becoming Valmiki (a Hindu sage) devotees, the women cling to polytheism; some men follow old religious forms and others are becoming skeptical. The desire of the young men is to join the new middle class rather than to follow the traditional caste system, a fact which itself suggests the measure of change coming about in village India.

No doubt the caste system and the joint family (which is responsible for familial rites and obligations) maintain the stability of the traditional religious beliefs. Some of these like food taboos, non-killing of certain animals (slaughter of cows and monkeys is specially forbidden), and belief in a divinely ordained destiny (*bhāgya* or fate) may be dysfunctional to the national goal of development. Others, like beliefs in renunciation (*vāṇaprastha* and *Sannyāsa* stages) and rebirth which foster quietism rather than activism, may serve as a temporary cushion against the shock felt by villagers when they compare their actual achievement under the present government with their induced secular aspirations. But, as we have shown earlier, religious roles and sacred values can be revaluated in terms of the changing needs of the Indian society. There is no founder or leader of Hinduism and no established church whose authority could be invoked against such revaluations. The Vedas are a revealed body of principles and knowledge, subject to an infinite variety of interpretations, and the *Smrtis* do not enjoin the primacy of any one scripture over another. It may be noted that some of these scriptures lean more toward activism, while others are oriented toward pacifism and other-worldiness.

THE DEVELOPMENTAL VARIANT

The developmental variant comprises a complex of factors, generally economic, but also political, administrative, and psychological. Economic growth refers to "the deepening flow of incomes and the widening flow of production" (Heilbroner 1963:53); and, although this may sometimes be achieved faster under a totalitarian regime, there is a growing consciousness that democracy is more important than economic growth. The administrative machinery needed to maintain order and stability in a society and to make rational decisions with regard to economic activities is considered a prerequisite for national development. Also in order to make the great ascent to economic prosperity and make it self-sustaining, people have to be trained to be innovators, rational decision-makers and seekers of individual gains. The last point however raises a problem, which is often ignored, overlooked, or minimised. We would like to consider it briefly.

Fow people would have any objection to creating more goods for more people and ordering national intitutions in such a way that they may help in the industrialisation of the country. However, when it is suggested that the way to do it is to scrap important indigenous values which may be felt to be inimical to the present ways of initiating and sustaining economic development (Kapp 1963;16 ff), some people's cyebrows go up—and, we believe, not without valid reason. For economic growth is merely a means to a larger goal, which is the conservation and enhancement of civilisational life and values of a group, a community, a society, or a nation.

In this context, "modernisation" is a term whose meaning is not always clear, even to the specialist. We will scrutinise the definition of a specialist, Milton J. Esman, who says:

> Modernisation implies the acceptance of values and norms which are consistent with modern science, their gradual diffusion throughout the society; their assimilation into patterns of behaviour, and the emergence and distribution of new functions required to implement new social purposes [Esman 1962:27].

There are two elements in this definition which need special attention. These elements are "values and norms which are consistent with modern science" and "new social purposes". As modern science expands its purview, it explains more and more the causation of physical, chemical, biological, social and psychological phenomena. However, it cannot displace or disprove the supernatural or the divine, which alone provides solace or comfort to the believer, especially when he is faced with a personal crisis. It is possible that sciences can create "new social purposes", whereby the metaphysical and the supernatural may be forced to withdraw to more limited space on a person's psychological horizon, but they cannot completely displace them. Sometimes, the ethics which flow from certain metaphysical conceptions can be at odds with scientific explanation of behaviour, and in such cases, a compromise will be necessary. In the wake of industrialisation, prevalence of rationality in society will have to be accepted as an important value, but that does not necessitate the dogma that all actions must be judged in terms of efficiency alone. Human beings, unlike the parts of a machine, have emotions; and they seek gratifications which are not always of an instrumental nature. Where sacred values are involved, "social purposes" fostered by industrialisation need constantly to be watched and evaluated.

The development variant suggests that economic rationality as an ethic, scientific temperament as an attitude, and adequate institutional base for growth are necessary for the modernisation of a country. The developmental imperatives, however, do not necessarily dictate that all values should be geared to the economic growth of the society; and yet, this simple but important point is often lost sight of in this great debate.

Indian Imperatives

In the case of India, we will first note the developmental factors, which may be affected by the religious variant in a limited way only. Then we will present certain hypotheses about the interactions of religion and development.

The expanison or contraction of natural resources of the nation generally depends more on geophysical characteristics, on societal will to exploit them, on whether there is talent available to harness them, on the educational framework, on the geographic boundary (which may be changed as in the creation of the separate state of Pakistan out of India in 1947), on the maintenance of law and order, and sometimes on international aid and assistance than on religious factors. Food taboo of some sort being universal would, indeed, be a general exception to the above case.[4]

The ratio of people to resources is another important factor in economic growth. Population expansion and contraction depends on reproduction rate, gains due to immigration, loses due to emigration, and deaths due to natural causes and disasters. Here also one does not see any special proclivity on the part of Hinduism to influence these adversely against national goals. A son is needed to offer oblations to the ancestors, and this may somewhat skew the curve of birth rates if every parent wants a son. Birth control is acceptable (except to Roman Catholics and some others in India), and religious massacres are receding in the past. Infanticide seems to have vanished; and, although widow remarriage now acceptable even to upper castes may add to births, delayed marriage (especially helped by the education of women) and the unfortunate dowry system will perhaps cancel the net gain in this respect.

The creation of a monetised economy and the improvement of production and distribution factors are some of the basic problems of any developing nation. The Hindu religious system traditionally provides a special class, the *Vaiśya* to conduct business activities. In fact, the mercantile enterprises of India benefited from the prudence and specialised skills of *Vaiśya*, *Mārwarīs*, *Jains*—all incorporated into the Hindu *varna* system—as well as the *Parsees*. But what is important to note here is that no caste of Hindus is forbidden to enter into industrial economic roles of productive or distributive nature nor is it enjoined on a person to abnegate the role of a good consumer as a householder.

As far as the institutions for the initiation and the stabilisation of the process of economic growth are concerned, we believe that the prerequisites exist in modern India. There is an articulate leadership; a well-trained civil service; respect for law and order; a growing middle class; an expanding educational system; and a well developed mass media, which inform, guide, lead and challenge the people. Given the present determination of the national leaders in political and business fields and the co-operation of the people, there is no reason why India cannot "take off" for the great ascent toward industrialisation and prosperity.

HINDUISM AND DEVELOPMENT: SOME HYPOTHESES

In view of lack of adequate empirical data, we would like to present a series of propositions which seem to be true, but which can be tested as hypotheses on the relationship between Hinduism and the development of India.

1. Hinduism permits transvaluation of ethics and social behaviour in the context of the changing needs of the society, but if the transvaluation is to succed it must give primacy to spiritual and ethical matters.

2. Some transvaluations in the past have given the individual an important place in the social scheme of things. The individual's social and spiritual freedom cannot be ultimately circumscribed because he is supreme in his own right and autonomous in his standing (*Ātman* is Brahman, *i e.*, Self is God), according to an important tenet of High Hinduism.

3. The Hindu ethics prescribe the realisation of self in the service of others (*samastī men vyakti*), as well as of God; and conversely, society is valued only if it gives dignity to man (*vyaktī men samastī*) in his daily living.

4. In sanctioning the caste system, Hinduism had made provision for different secular orientations and behaviour for

different people. The revaluation of the social order forced by the industrialisation of society may change the values of the caste system, but it will not undermine the sacred roots of Hindu society.

5. Achievement orientation will not have a disorganising influence on individuals because the resulting change would be considered equitable by the group, provided the revaluation involved is legitimised by those leaders who operate in the larger context of High Hinduism.

6. Hinduism is generally receptive to material growth, because it helps a person to perform his sacred duties more adequately.

Now a few propositions about the changes we forsee in the religious sphere of the Hindus as the national Five Year Plans advance the economic growth of India :

(i) The concepts of *Ātman* (sacredness of self) and *īstadevatā* (personalised God) will be retained by the Hindus even if many other philosophical concepts lose their valence.

(ii) The inferior role of woman in the sacred sphere will be difficult to change, inspite of the enhancement of her position in the society through education and equal partnership with men in secular affairs. (The ritual subordination of women is deeply ingrained in the Hindu sacred order.)

(iii) The prescriptions concerning food and intercaste association will gradually breakdown.

(iv) The *brāhman* will be relegated to the position of a parish priest rather than that of an inherently superior person (whose first ancestor mythically emanated from the mouth of *virāt puruṣa*, the creator of the universe).

(v) Esteem for the person who shows "selfless action" in business, politics, or other mundane affairs will continue to be great, inspite of the growth of secular education and interest group-oriented politics.

(vi) The twin principles of unity in diversity and diversity in unity will emphasise tolerance, but will delay the emergence of a unitary national bond which can cement the divisive factors and conflicting factions in the Indian body politic today.

CONCLUSION

Hinduism is a religion which encompasses both the sacred and secular orders of the society. In order to fully understand the range of permissive behaviour allowed by Hinduism, historical research has to be done on India's past, relating to the development of High Hinduism traditional scriptures and commentaries on them) and Popular Hinduism (actual values, beliefs, and actions of the people). Empirical data on the present also needs to be collected. Hindu ethics seem cosmopolitan enough to generate values pertinent to development (Singer 1956: 10). However, such values have to be articulated and re-emphasised by dedicated leaders. The new ethic on industrial development will not gain primacy, if India's past is belittled and ridiculed, and if economic values are given major precedence over spiritual values.

India needs more entrepreneurs,[5] but not necessarily more people with high achievement motive. It is possible that the seekers of spiritual truths may be quite high achievers, except that their efforts are channelised in an other worldly direction. A society like India, which has started on an ambitious road to planning, should be able to plan its resources, institutions and goals in such a way that both the material and spiritual needs of the people are duly met. Psychological determinism is as untenable as social darwinism in the evolution of a self-realising society.

FOOT NOTES

1. It is interesting to note that this aspect of the question, *i.e.*, the possible transsubstantiation of the secular in sacred terms has not

been clarified in an attempt by Robert N. Bellah in working out a typology of world religions in evolutionary terms (Bellah 1964). Another student of religion concedes that "Nothing is being done [by the sociologist] on the interrelationship between religious ideas and the values of the economic order" [Glock 1959:176].

2. These categories have been arrived at inductively by examining the literature and the personal experience of the author. The vernacular names are used by the people themselves.

3. David G. Mandelbaum has meaningfully separated the transcendental and pragmatic aspects of religious worship. However, the question of overlap between these functions even in "more fully differentiated" religions like Hindusim, has not been discussed by him (Mandelbaum 1966).

4. Much has been written about the question of the ban on the slaughter of the "holy cow" in India. For rebuttal of the arguments of the economic developers, see Marvin Harris' article, "The Myth of The Sacred Cow" (Harris 1965).

5. David C. McClelland has worked assiduously on the problem of creating entrepreneurs for the developing nations (McClelland 1961).

REFERENCES

Arapura, John G.
1953 East, West, and Professor Northrop. New India 4:5-12.

Bellan, Robert N.
1964 Religious Evolution. American Sociological Review 29:358-374.

Cohn, Bernard S.
1955 The Changing Status of a Depressed Caste. *In* Village India Studies in the Little Community. Mckim Mariott, ed., Chicago, The University of Chicago Press.

Esman, Milton J.
1962 Institution Building in National Development. International Development Review 4:27-30. (Vol. 4 No-4, Decmber 1962).

Glock, Charles Y.
1959 The Sociology of Religion. *In* Sociology Today Problems and Prospects. Robert K. Merton, et.al., New York, Basic Books.

Gough, E. Kathleen
1955 The Social Structure in a Tanjore Village. *In* Village India

Studies in the Little Community. Mckim Mariott, ed., Chicago, The University of Chicago Press.

Harper, Edward B. Ed.

1964 Religion in South Asia. Seattle, University of Washington Press.

Harris, Marvin

1965 The Myth of the Sacred Cow. *In* Man, Culture and Animals: The Role of Animals in Human Ecological Adjustments. Anthony Leeds and Andrew P. Vayda, eds., Washington D.C., American Association for the Advancement of Science. Publication No. 78.

Heilbroner, Robert L.

1963 The Great Ascent: The Struggle for Economic Development In Our Time. New York, Harper & Row. Harper Torchbook Edition, 1963.

Hook, Sidney

1962 Philosophy and Human Conduct. *In* Philosophy and Culture: East and West. Charles A. Moore, ed., Honolulu, University of Hawaii Press.

Hu, Shih

1962 The Scientific Spirit and Method in Chinese Philosophy. *In* Philosophy and Culture: East and West. Charles A Moore, ed., Honolulu, University of Hawaii Press.

Kapp, K. William

1963 Hindu Culture Economic Development and Economic Planning in India. New York, Asia Publishing House.

Lenski. Gerhard

1961 The Religious Factor: A Sociologist's Inquiry. Garden City, New York, Doubleday & Company. Anchor Book Edition, 1963.

Lewis, Oscar

1958 Village Life in Northern India. New York, Randon House. Vintage Book Edition, 1965.

Mahar, Pauline Moller

1960 Changing Religious Practices Of An Untouchable Caste. Economic Development and Cultural Change 8: 279-287.

Mandelbaum, David G.

1966 Transcendental and Pragmatic Aspects of Religion. American Anthropologist 68: 1174-1191.

Marriott, Mckim

1955 Little Communities In An Indigenous Civilization. *In* Village India Studies in the Little Community. Mckim Marriett, ed., Chicago, The University of Chicago Press.

McClelland, David C.

1961 The Achieving Society. New York, D. Van Nostrand Company.

Northrop, F.S.C.

1944 The Complementary Emphasis of Eastern Initiative and Western Scientific Philosophy. *In* Philosophy—East and West. Charles A. Moore, ed., Princeton, Princeton University Press.

1946 The Meeting of East and West. New York, The Macmillan Company.

1952 The Taming of the Nations. New York, The Macmillan Company.

Opler, Morris E.

1950 Village Life In North India. Chicago, The Delphian Society.

Radhakrishan, S.

1962 The Indian Approach to the Religious Problem. *In* Philosophy and Culture: East and West. Charles A Moore, ed., Honolulu, University of Hawaii Press.

Raju, P.T.

1962 Religion and Spiritual Values in Indian Thought. *In* Philosophy and Culture: East and West. Charles A. Moore, ed., Honolulu, University of Hawaii Press.

Redfield, Robert

1955 The Social Organisation of Tradition. Far Eastern Quarterly 15: 13-21.

1956 Peasant Society and Culture. Chicago, The University of Chicago press.

Singer, Milton

1956 A Postscript to India's Cultural Values and Economic Development: A Discussion. Economic Development and Cultural Change 7: 1-12,

Srinivas, M.N.

1956 A Note on Sanskritization and Westernization. Far Eastern Quarterly 15: 481-496.

Weber, Max

1930 The Protestant Ethic and the Spirit of Capitalism. New York, Charles Scribner.

Werkmeister, W.H.

1962 Scientism and the Problem of Man. *In* Philosophy and Culture: East and West. Charles A. Moore, ed., Honolulu, University of Hawaii Press.

INDIA'S MODERNISATION : EVOLUTIONARY OR REVOLUTIONARY ?

3

India's Modernisation : Evolutionary or Revolutionary?

INTRODUCTION

INDIA has many faces and modernisation is construed from many points of view. I will try to explore first the civilisational tradition of India and then I will put forth a multi-dimensional view of modernisation, which has been explored in my recent book, *The Sociology and Politics of Development : A Theoretical Study*.

First, about the civilisation that is India. The one problem that impinges on India's modernisation is its diversified culture. India is a subcontinent in the true sense ; it has the multiplicity of Europe and yet the unity of the United States. Tribes, castes, linguistic groups, religious denominations dot its regions and yet a unity prevails in its villages and cities, which is unmatched elsewhere except perhaps in the United States. Modernisation, in the sense of Westernisation or the "socialistic pattern of society" as it was called by Jawaharlal Nehru, shows a new thrust in the traditional body politic of India.

What is the framework of the traditional polity of India? I would put it in terms of the concept of "unity in diversity" (*vyakti men samasti*). An individual encapsulates the cosmos of the whole, just as the whole or the community represents the diversity of individual natures and propensities of action. The Vedas (with the primacy given to Rgveda) posit unity of thought, which then went into diverse directions in the Brahmanas, Puranas, Vedantas and other scriptures codifying forms of worship, ritual, philosophy and cosmology. If the Ramayana represents the unity and strengths of the ideal polity, the Mahabharata depicts the diversity and creativity of political life. The Gita enjoins Karma Yoga (life of action), but the Vedas preach four elements of such life (the *purushārthas*, as they are called), viz., *dharma* (laws), *artha* (possessions), *kāma* (desires), and *moksha* (renunciation and release). Thus, the active life of a householder, the key to modernisation, is not to be shunned or discredited in any way.

If the key to modernisation is the unity of a people, then it exists in the civilisational life of India as indicated above. However, if one is looking for nationhood or national integration, that sense is still weak, although gaining in strength since the early years of this century. The traditional polity has been reinterpreted in India throughout history. In recent times, Mohandas Karamchand Gandhi and Deendayal Upadhyaya, among others, have emphasised civilisational values. However, men like M.N. Roy and Subhas Chandra Bose tried to impose a different set of principles, the former guided by Karl Marx's thesis and the latter by the heroic traditions of the East and the West. These two contemporary idealists have strong following in the ideological core of the Indian body politic today. Any consideration of India's modernisation must contend with the pool of wisdom and ideology bequeathed to it by these thinkers as well as many others like them.

Models of Modernisation

What is modernisation ? Common sensically it implies two questions : Who wants what good things of life ? And, who can get how much of these things ? We social scientists spend all our life answering these simple but vexing questions.

Economic growth and nation-building have been two activities discussed most in the modernisation literature. In the course of a decade, I had the opportunity to examine four hundred books and one thousand articles about the modernisation process of about a hundred countries. What stood out in my mind is that there are two viable models of modernisation for any country. One I call the capitalist model and the other, the socialist model.

I would like to outline the basic elements of these models. Under capitalism, private ownership of the means of production will continue forever, labour will sell its services in a market situation, the state will guarantee the accumulation of profit, and all private gains by individuals can be bequeathed to their heirs. Under socialism, private ownership of the means of production is abolished; labour, as a class determines the level of production; non-familial labour is not available for personal profit; and any private property which can be converted into independent means of production, cannot be inherited.

I have presented above the *weltanschauungs* of the capitalist and the socialist models. The grounds of their viability and application cannot be questioned just because some deviations from the model may occur.

Evolutionary Future

I would like now to discuss six different aspects of contemporary social life in India, *viz.*, national integration, urbanisation, economic change, political direction, education and development of science and technology.

First, the question of national integration. There is a consciousness among most Indians of all regions of a sense of nationhood, what with eight general elections for the Indian Parliament and several patriotic wars, which India has fought after its independence from the British rule in 1947.

National unity asserts itself in times of natural disasters, *e.g.*, flood or famine, or under conditions of social conflict, like the Hindu-Muslim riots or linguistic and tribal uprisings. It is reaffirmed also in national calamities, such as India-China War. There are no doubt costs of nation-building which every multiglot nation must pay. However, the civilisational imperatives of India, *e.g.*, the reigning principle of unity in diversity help in times of distress. I am, however, not suggesting that unity is easily gained, if only because the formula for such unity varies from one ideological group to another. I wish to emphasise this point, because modernisation is *par excellence* an ideological issue in all countries.

The planners of India continuously guided the nation in the direction of pragmatism, what with adopting the pursuit of "mixed economy" and nationalisation of some key sectors of the economy and the infusion of massive aids from both the capitalist and the Soviet countries. The emphasis on early industrialisation was beneficial on two counts, one, the movement in the direction of mass education, and, two, creating the infrastructure for economic growth, leading eventually to exports of goods and technology both to industrial as well as industrialising nations, and especially to Africa and the Middle East.

We come next to the question of urbanisation. The growth of urbanisation is not so marked in its scope as in its ideology in India. Despite over thirty years of developmental planning, only 22% of India's population is urban; some of India's cities have inflated beyond their capacities in providing employment for their residents. However, the urban way of life is seeping into the villages, what with transistor radios, moving cinema houses in rural fairs, and community development programmes of one kind or another. Also every prosperous family wants to send at least one son to the city for education and employment.

The middle-sized cities act as the buffer between urban life and the rural life of India. The big cities are generally ridden with poverty and insecurity, except for the rich and the employed; on the other hand, the villages no longer continue their centuries-old style of "plain living and high thinking." The peasants dispossessed by the landlords are the bane of the villages and of the cities, where they eventually migrate to. It is in this context that plans for decentralisation of the economy and the growth of Agro-Industries seem very urgent as Jayaprakash Narayan, among others, has pointed out. The Janata government, in its short-lived regime, had started with some pious intentions and small beginnings; the present government hopefully may also give impetus to several beneficient programmes of rural employment.

The area of economic change deserves a paper by itself. The problems of population growth everywhere impinge on the pace of economic growth. It should be noted, however, that if the population explosion was not so massive in India, for instance, adding the numerical weight of the whole population of the United States in the last thirty years to India's already overburdened population, the economic usufruct would have been quite satisfying for its teeming millions. The patrimonial attitude of the government toward both management and labour in the factories has served the country well so far. What India needs from its economists is to provide guidelines for establishing a viable Agro-Industrial society, which so far does not exist anywhere.

The political life of India is thriving, but perhaps ready for a big change. One does not know if a Soviet type revolution will ever come to India. I have noticed recently a growth in the study of peasant movements by social scientists of India, partly dictated by the endemic conflicts between the have's and the have not's of rural India. The political parties of today are viable but lack leadership, except for those which are counted as Left or Right parties. The organisational wing of mass parties is inefficient, to say the least. The judicial, the executive, and the military branches of the government are sophisticated and competent, but the lack of national political leadership in the recent past may eventually lead to a need for change in India's constitution. I would not be surprised if a Presidential form of government like that in the United States or even France may come soon and, if so, it may be for the better. The election of Rajiv Gandhi as the new Prime Minister is a new quotient in the matter.

The educational system of India has shown some resourcefulness considering the fact that it was introduced by the British to keep the nation in bondage. The growth of liberal arts, however, has not been liberal enough to incorporate the ideas inherited from India's own civilisational past. The sciences and engineering fields have done much better and so has medicine in terms of fulfilling some of India's needs. However, their graduates must be deployed in rural areas, so that their own know how for solving the country's problems and catering to the rural population may increase. The brain drain to the West is mostly for self-serving purposes of the graduates, but that to the African and other developing nations can be considered as serving altruism as well as opportunism. The scientific laboratories and the medical research institutes in India are a definite boon to the country as well as for other developing countries.

India's modernisation is at crossroads today. India does not know if it should continue with its capitalistic mode of development, perhaps tinkering with elements of public enterprises or if it should go in the Soviet direction. If there is going to be a Soviet-type revolution, I suspect that it would be preceded by military dictatorship. However, the framework of Indian civilisation is such that the society cannot remain closed forever. The independence of thought in its traditional mode of existence will militate against making a shambles of open society, which India is and has been through the millennia.

The recent tradition of India, at least from the time of its independence, has been one of seeking stability in the midst of massive change. If the population gets stabilised through birth control and its growth rate decreases, if the educational system is revamped by the introduction of the indigenous intellectual and artistic traditions of India in the curriculum, and by moving in the direction of self-help in the states and perhaps delinking education from some kind of jobs, if the economists and the national leaders put their energies together in accelerating the growth of Agro-Industries, if the political situation gets optimistic either through realignment of parties in the direction of a two party system or through changes in the Indian constitution, if science and engineering as well as medicine are made to serve all the people and not merely the elites, and if the diverse leadership in the country from the village to the national levels realises the promise of a united India, one can see a ray of hope on the horizon. These are big ifs, whose answers must come from those who may dare to deal with them. For me, India's modernisation is only partial, until the physical and mental poverty of its submerged half, the people who have been called "below poverty line" by the economists and "the lowliest and the lost" by Rabindranath Tagore, is erased in the coming years.

Revolutionary Future ?

So far I have given an analysis of the Indian situation from an evolutionary and, what seems to me in retrospect as, the bourgeois liberal point of view. Let me now don my other hat, that of a theorist on revolution. I was a close associate of Jayaprakash Narayan, whose Socialist Study Circle of two dozen people I was fortunate enough to join when I was a young man in college. We read Karl Marx and V.I. Lenin together and then wrangled with problems of revolution from the anarchist, the socialist, and the capitalist points of view.

I should now make a few prognoses for revolution in India. I would like to do it with a bold brush but perhaps with what some may call shaky facts. I have always felt that those who believe in revolution create it, those who don't, like us social scientists, live with it. I do not know who will create revolution in India but I have reasons to suspect that someone will. The following analysis pertains to the grounds of revolution, if and when it comes to India, and the results thereof.

I think that in a successful revolution, there is a congruence of thesis and praxis, somewhat along the lines proposed by Karl Marx, V.I. Lenin, and Mao Zedong. The thesis in India is that elitism and equalitarianism are in dialectical relationship. The praxis consists of the fact that the class structure of Western capitalism bequeathed to India by the British rule is in conflict with the forces unleashed by the Indian constitution as well as also with some of the equity-seeking values in a segment of the traditional body politic of India. A part of the praxis also consists of the conflict between the caste system and the equalitarian ethos adopted by the emerging political system as well as by the mass media, especially the movies, as they mould public opinion. The detalis of the thesis and the praxis in India will take a whole book to elaborate on, just as the nature of their dialectical relationships will be a continuing topic of discussion among Marxist and other Leftist intellectuals.

I wish to present here an evaluation of the revolutionary situation in India today, which may lead to a successful socialist revolution. The one party rule in India at the centre gave in to multi-party confusion during the Janata regime and then the country again went back to one party, or, one may say, one person rule. There is a diversity of opinion among Indian intellectuals about the political destiny of India in the coming decades. In the turmoil of recent years, the Communist parties of India have consolidated their hold, although still on a minority of the masses. The programmes of changing the condition of the poor in Kerala and West Bengal, both states ruled by Communist parties for some time, have succeeded markedly. The success of the equalitarian programmes of these two states will give fillip to revolutionary forces in other states as well in the future.

On the national level, if the political parties fail to rule the country, which is the way it seemed for a while, the military may move in, but the military will never be able to consolidate its regime. The chaotic condition of the capitalist regimes as most of India's recent regimes have been at the centre or in the states, or the vulnerabilities of the military rule, if it ever comes to India, at the hands of the multi-regional multi-credal peoples of India will, in my judgment, give additional push to the revolutionary forces in the country.

What are these revolutionary forces? One is the peasant movements flourishing now in all parts of the country.

When the peasant movements cannot be stopped, and as they gain momentum in contemporary Indian life, someone or selected few members of one or other organised movement will silently but surely gain national leadership and come to the helm of Indian political affairs. When such a person or persons appear on the scene, India's masses will be ready to follow him, her, or them. After all, for more than two decades of contemporary Indian history, Mahatma Gandhi, a simple man, the naked fakir, as he was called by Winston Churchill, had a following which kings and dictators envied around the world.

My next point is about the direction of that struggle, which, when it is ready to shape the destiny of the nation, has to be called a revolution. The blueprints of a socialist type of revolution have already been laid down by Lenin and Mao. Additional blueprints are available in the varied writings of Jayaprakash Narayan. The details may vary, the strategy may be somewhat different, but the goal is the same. In ideological terms, it is scientific socialism. If a Socialist revolution comes to India, the country may decide to isolate itself, as China did for over a quarter century, or it may remain open to all influences, like Yugoslavia has done, provided the socialist *weltanschauung*, outlined earlier, is not destroyed in that process.

The socialist route to modernisation for India implies that there will be a countrywide revolution, perhaps brought about by regional revolts gaining strength and accelerating in tempo in a very short time. The national struggle will adopt an ideology of *socialist struggle against classes and reactionaries* and will constantly move in the direction of establishing economic equality for all citizens of the country. In this struggle, the equities based on the capitalist system, *e.g.*, rights to private property, will be deemphasised or perhaps even abolished.

I have indicated in my book that in any revolutionary struggle, ideology comes first. However, after revolution, there must be a comprehensive plan of national reconstruction. The grounds for such a plan have been sketched out by me. At the minimum, it will need goal maintenance, which in institutional terms means abolition of classes and the avoidance of any policy which may end up in the reemergence of new classes. The leaders of socialist society (in the Marxist sense) must guard their ramparts as much against class interests as the leaders of capitalist society guard against encroachment by the masses or any defiant government or intelligentsia. A socialist revolution for India is not a dream. It is within the purview of reality, if history rolls on with accelerated pace in the same direction as it has done since the seventies.

I have emphasized above the grounds for the emergence of revolution. It is difficult to give an exact blueprint now unless the forces mentioned earlier gain momentum. Peasant revolts, Left trade union movements, student rebellions (*e.g.*, Chchatra Sangharsha Samitis), people's revolts (Jan Morchas) may all coalesce together and form a network of unified national movement moving in the direction of transforming the Indian Union into a Union of Indian Soviet Republics. It is hard to predict when it will come to be. But it is reasonable to assume that some other organisations, such as the successful cooperatives of India, which can avoid manipulation by the agents of the government, the panchayats of West Bengal type, the network of rural leadership which keeps pressure on the government to make the rural bodies serve efficiently the rural people in Kerala, will provide added impetus to the revolutionary movement. In the ensuing struggle, caste and religious institutions as well as the governmental and political framework will be first made powerless and then ignored or bypassed by the revolutionary leaders. Since more than half the Indian population lives below the poverty line, they may not show much resistance to revolutionary change.

The urban population, especially the white collar class, is peculiarly powerless in the face of an ideologieal movement. The middle class always likes to join hands with whoever may be in power. It is only the rich capitalists and landholders who, with the help of a section of the bureaucracy, police and the military, may stand in the way of revolutionary transformation. However, if the lean structure of the present Indian political institutions and the guiding light of India's massive constitution start to fade away in the face of current inflation, unemployment, abominable poverty at the side of massive luxury of the few, and social chaos, no one is to gain but the incipient forces which will carry the revolution onwards. The bourgeois newspapers and other mass media may give some opposition to the forces for radical change, but they will have their counterparts in the camp of revolution. A further projection of the future of India's revolution will be merely an intellectual exercise beyond this point.

One final word now. If India sticks to its present capitalist path of modernisation and the political leadership crisis remains as it has been in the recent past, it will go through many more crises of emergency rules, secessionist movements and even military regimes In the process, it may perhaps become a new periphery of a Western capitalist core country, from which situation it has tried to extricate itself after attaining independence. As to the future, whether India will continue on its capitalist route to modernisation or go the revolutionary way, only time can tell.

INDIANS AS NEW ETHNICS IN THE UNITED STATES: A THEORETICAL NOTE

4

Indians as New Ethnics in the United States: A Theoretical Note*

A RECENT visitor from India asked me, "How are the ethnic Indians doing in New York? I understand America is a melting pot, which is heating up to become a boiling cauldron. What are the chances of survival of the Indians here? Are they happy?" These are big questions which arise in the mind of a visiting Indian as much as in the thinking of resident Indians. Only a sociological look at these problems can afford an insight for mature judgement.

The Indians can be classified as New Ethnics because their migration to the United States started first as a trickle in 1895 and reached its peak of 5,000 immigrants at San Francisco in 1910.[1] These working class Indians formed enclaves in California. In 1922, there were 2600 Indians in the United States, but in 1940, only 2400 were counted. Of the more than 3000 Indians in 1950, the student population was 1500.[2] The rigidity of immigration laws gave a quota of 100 Indians annually to India in 1946, which was not changed until the mid-1960's. Then started the second wave of migration. There are over half a million Indians in the United States

* Reprinted from Parmatma Saran and Edwin Eames (editors), *The New Ethnics Asian Indians in the United States*, New York, Friderick, A Praeger, 1980.

today, of which about 50,000 reside in the larger Metropolitan New York area.[3]

Few Indians know that the United States Supreme Court, in a decision in 1923, disallowed the claim of a Punjabi Sikh to be considered a member of the white (caucasian) race.[4] This decision was hailed by the California press, which was then agitating against the rights of orientals to be considered full-fledged citizens of the United States. In fact, the earlier perception of the immigrant Indian was that of the member of a "lower breed" in the mind of the authorities as well as of many Americans.[5]

The new wave of Indian immigrants, which started in 1965, has brought mostly professional and middle class people from India, and this along with the international fame of Gandhi and the contributions of India after its independence in 1947 in humanitarian and international causes, may have changed the picture quite a bit. Although no surveys are available, it is reasonable to assume that Indians are not considered "coloured" in the United States today as they are in Britain.[6] In England, Indians are a racial category, in the United States they are an ethnic group.

ETHNIC GROUP

What is an ethnic group ? It is important to understand what an ethnic group is in order to evaluate the position of Indians in the United States. In the International Encyclopedia of the Social Sciences, an ethnic group is defined as "a distinct category of the population in a larger society whose culture is usually different from its own."[7] In this sense, the Indian population as a whole in the United States does qualify as an ethnic group, because its culture is different from that of the United States. However, it should be noted that subcommunities of Indians, e.g., Punjabis, Gujaratis, South Indians, Bengalis, do not form ethnic groups either in

India or in the United States. In India, they do not have a distinct culture as contrasted from the Indian culture (in terms of the above definition),[8] and in the United States, the subcommunities or subcultural groups are neither perceived nor recognised by Americans for purposes of categorisation or interaction. In fact, this line of reasoning is supported by the fact that there is no indigenous word for "ethnic group" in Hindi or anyone of the major languages of India, as far as I know.

Why is it then that the regional or linguistic groups of India are called ethnic groups and books are written about them ? It is because the terms ethnic group, minority group and subculture are often used interchangeably, and sometimes, with a good deal of confusion.[9] Social scientists have sometimes different perspectives on the same phenomenon depending on the problem which interests them. If the issue is one of assimilation, then the three terms can perhaps be used interchangeably. However, we believe one should make a distinction in talking about ethnic groups in India and in the United States. All persons with Indian ancestry constitute the Indian ethnic group in the United States. But in India, groups which suffer from some handicap like the scheduled castes and scheduled tribes, should be categorised as minority groups rather than ethnic groups, and other groups based on religion such as Anglo-Indians, Jains, Sikhs and Parsees should be called subcultures. Although there are important overlaps between minorities and subcultures, the two should be kept separate for classification purposes. An ethnic group is altogether a different category than a minority or a subculture, if one is interested in the theoretical implications of these terms.

For elucidation, it would help to examine the status of the term ethnic group in India. In the first place, it does not mean a thing for the non-English speaking population, which may be as high as 98 per cent. Usually, the villager relates to a stranger in terms of *jāti* (a subdivision of the caste order), *kāl* (time or the period about which one is talking), and *pātra* ("inheritor of values" or person). Then, place of inhabitation, or *sthāna* (place) or *desh* (country) has also a meaning, although not always the same for all people. Thus, in ancient India, a distinction was made between the *Āryāvarta* (the place where the *Āryans* lived) and the rest of the country, which included the Deccan plateau. Since *Āryāvarta* was considered a valued place of residence in antiquity, the South Indians of today often react with negative sentiments against some of the values and the scriptural injunctions of North Indians, who are presumed to be descendents of the *Āryan* tribes living in *Āryāvarta.* As compared to the contextual nodes of interaction in terms of *jāti*, *kāl*, *pātra* and *sthān*, there is the textual category of the *varna* (literally "colour") order, which distinguishes one man from another.

In our judgement, the *varna* order has four referents. First, it is the ranked, hierarchial categories of Brahman (Priest), Kshatriya (Warrior and Scribe), Vaishya (Trader, Artisan) and Shudra (Worker) lineages. Second, it is a category of valued behaviour prescribed for each group as, for instance, enunciated in the Manusmriti (the laws of Manu). Third, it is a collectivity of stratified groups having different rights and perquisites in the traditional moral and legal systems. And fourth, it is a composite of ethnic type groups which have different ancestry, value systems, and political outlooks as well as modes of participation in the body politic.[10] Only in the last case, if at all, can the *varna* order be seen as comprising ethnic groups.

Besides the *varna* classification of peoples in India, there are other classifications, based on religion, sectarianism, language, region, race, and what have you. Some of these groups qualify as ethnic groups. But to put all of these classifications in one category and call them ethnic group, does not do justice to the case. As we said earlier, in India most people do not know what an ethnic group is, and those who know English, when faced with the question, "What ethnic group do you belong to ?" may select some of the above mentioned categories for answering it.

In the American situation, the term ethnic group refers to a number of characteristics, such as differentiation by race, religion or national origin, as Milton M. Gordon has demonstrated.[11] For our purposes here, we would like to adopt the definition of J. Milton Yinger, who states : "An ethnic group, as I will use this term, is a segment of a larger society, whose members are thought, by themselves and/or others, to have a common origin and to share important segments of a common culture and who, in addition, participate in shared activities in which the common origin and culture are significant ingredients. It is important to distinguish a sociologically and psychologically important ethnicity from one that is only administrative or classificatory."[12] The people, originating in India and residing in the United States, do qualify as an ethnic group in the social structure of the United States. Both self perception as well as societal characterisation as ethnic, the two main features of Yinger's definition, are present.[13]

We will now look at the various dimensions of ethnicity of Indians and their relationship to "ethnic renaissance" in the United States.[14] The ethnicity of Indians in the United States today is very much a function of the "ethnic renaissance" of the present times. The literature on ethnic movements is voluminous and we do not intend to go into it here. Our thesis, simply stated, is that as the United States moves to higher stages of advanced industrialism, there is a need for man to escape from the clutches of machine, technology and computers. One aspect of the new ethnicity derives from a reaction to the standardisation of life and values in American society. The other aspect of ethnicity is dictated by the opening up of the American system to the equitable needs and demands of the minorities and subcultural groups. Job opportunities in the economic sphere, a modicum of respect for one's heritage, and the pursuit of excellence in ethnic arts and culture are all related to ethnic resurgence today.

THE INDIAN ETHNIC

Indians in the United States today are both perceived by the larger society as an ethnic category and they also see themselves in that light in various degrees. What an American thinks of an Indian when he meets him cannot be divorced from what the Americans think of India. In this respect, an earlier study documented a stereotype, which was more Kiplingese than real.[15] The maharajah, nabob, yogi, snake charmer, rope trick, sacred cow were all part of a syndrome characteristic of India, that was universally disliked in the United States. The book *Mother India*, published by Katherine Mayo in 1927, also focussed American attention in the same direction. It sold about 257,000 copies in 27 editions through the 1950's.[16]

The nether India, the India of "teeming millions" existing on subsistence economy, was later replaced in the mind of an American by the India of Gandhi, the "politician-saint," who combined the images of George Washington, Lincoln and Jesus, and the India of Nehru, one of "the three great statesmen of this century, along side Churchill and Roosevelt." Nehru was one of "the few leaders with a world view" in the minds of many an American.[17] But what about the Indians who came to study in the United States by the thousands and those who later migrated there in hundreds of thousands during the last decades? It appears that the general picture of an Indian in the thinking of an American is positive, *e.g.*, "charming, friendly, hospitable," with an admixture of criticism, such as, "holier-than-thou, hypocritical," and "unreliable."[18] It is a truism to say that most people in the world do not like foreigners, so even a little tilt in the direction of possessing positive traits speaks favourably for the position of Indians in the United States.

We would now like to examine the question : "are the Indians in the United States a community ?" The answer is a partial yes. The Indians are a commonalty, but not yet a community. In terms of group traits, they have a mode of thinking ("superiority—inferiority complex" or "garrulousness"),[19] which comes across easily to the Americans, who interact with them. Their speech, manner of dressing at home and food, as well as their somewhat fatalistic attitude toward life also stand out. Their customs and taboos (about eating beef or pork, or vegetarianism), their rites, ceremonies and forms of worship are rather unusual for Americans.

Their folklores, songs, jokes and forms of recreation including Indian movies are also different. The fads and fashions in wearing *sarees* and jewelry are, however, only noticeable to other Indians in the United States. The sense of pride and pain which they feel in matters affecting interpersonal relationship is sealed from an American's perception. because of his lack of understanding of the basic values of Indian civilisation. However, the professional nature of the Indian's job makes for frequent shifts in residence and thus community is difficult to form.

Most Indians in the United States are able to associate with each other, no matter what the linguistic, subcultural, caste or regional barrier may be at home. There is also a mutual acceptance of some of the values in which they may differ greatly in India. However, when it comes to marriage, they fall back on the Indian tradition. Many Indians, resident in the United States, go back to India to obtain a marriage partner ; although this is not to say that intermarriages between Indian subcultural groups in the United States and with Americans do not occur. All Indians prize social mobility for themselves as well as for their children in the United States and are willing to sacrifice personal comforts to enhance the life chances of the members of their nuclear and even joint families. Joint families generally form in the United States when parents come from India to reside with their children, or when brothers and other relatives decide to stay in the same household.

The developing sense of community among Indians in the United States often works as a barrier to their wishes for assimilation in the American society. In pursuit of the latter aim, some Indians openly boast of their membership in American social clubs and at the same time make it a point to publicise the fact that they have no Indian friends in the United States. Others, however, join their regional, linguistic or subcultural organisations to find friends and thus spend most of their leisure time in association with other Indians of their own kind. Some of these organisations are also a bridge to the Indian's contact with American civic and political organisations. Individual Americans quite often participate in the social life of Indian ethnic organisations. The dance, drama, music and even religious performances by Indians attract Americans as well as members from all subcultural groups of Indian origin.

It is with regard to the role of the women and children that one will have to seek an important clue to the assimilation of Indians in the American culture. The Indian women, by and large, are proud of wearing their *sarees*, although they are not loath to adopt Western dress when the occasion demands. The Indian children generally receive a higher dose of Indian culture from the mother rather than from the father, who is usually overworked on weekdays and overpressed to meet his Indian friends on weekends. The almost yearly family trek to India maintains one's cultural and familial links with India ; it may also be partly necessitated by a sense of loneliness among the adults. The Indian children adapt well to the life in the schools. They spend most of their time at home with parents, so there is no need for boy's or girl's clubs. Deliquency seems to be negligible at least in the present generation. There are no doubt some mental health problems for adults, but self esteem is generally high among Indian immigrants.

The proliferation of Indian organisations is dictated partly by cultural needs and partly by the fact that most Indian immigrants are professionals, who are also concerned about the socio-political life in India. To the extent that one's ties to India are continued, what with periodical visits back home, *Bhārat Darshan* (viewing India) as it is called, and what with ethnic newspapers (mostly concerned about news from India) and contacts with visiting Indians, to that degree Indians have less of a chance to move into the arena of American socio-political life. It is true that there are Indian organisations and groups that are relating themselves to American politics and civic life, but by and large, the opportunity to participate in American life is bypassed by most Indians.

The ideology which infuses Indians is the ideology of making India a cherished and prestigious country rather than making similar efforts for the advancement of American society. This ideology is conducive to social movements, but so far little has been coming out in that direction. Perhaps the overseas Indians, as they were called during India's rule by the British, were more politically active in earlier days because of necessity or of their wish to return home after independence.[20] Although the Indian immigrant of recent decades may have an open or subconscious desire to return to India some day, he does not think he can do much to influence the politics of India. At best, some token effort at social reform, such as decrying the custom of dowry or championing the cause of the *harijans* (untouchables) or "adopting a village"[21], may come out from the advices, letters and pronouncements of the Indians in the United States. The Indians are loath to convert their sentiments into reform or regeneration movements. The propagation of Khalistan by some Sikhs is a new phenomenon.

A section of Indians in the United States comes from the trading communities of Gujarat and Punjab, and this section may carry on its daily life and activities the same way as it does in India. Another section shows entrepreneurship, as the Sikhs from Punjab do, but, by and large, the Indian community is composed of the same heterogeneous mix of castes, subcultural values, and behaviour as one sees in the metropolises of India. One can almost say that the Indian enclaves in the United States (except for the old settlers of the Fresno valley in California) are a microcosm of the social structure of the Indian metropolis. However, none of them can be categorised as an underclass population, which vitiates Indian cities.

Some Indians have recently become involved in getting for the Indians the status of a minority group for purposes of the "affirmative action" programme and its implementation.[22] Another section of Indians is vocally opposed to it for fear of a backlash. This kind of involvement in American politics may perhaps have a lasting effect on the integration of Indians as an ethnic community in the United States and of the developing orientation of this community to the United States rather than to India.[23]

At a meeting of the leaders of the Indian community with the American press, someone complained that the American press was oblivious of the fact that half a million Indians lived in the United States. There was no news about them in the national press. At this, one lady from the press remarked, "you have done nothing wrong so far. Wait until you make a mistake and then you will surely hear from the press."[24] The leaders of the Indian community could not believe that somehow no news is good news.[25]

It is perhaps the professional qualifications and the rate of employment of the members of the Indian community, perhaps the leadership of India in Third World politics as well as its "non aligned" role in world politics, or perhaps the lack of interest on the part of Americans in the activities of a miniscule community in the American ethnic framework, that has given the Indians a chance to do whatever they are qualified to do professionally as well as socially in the United States. Also the "colour bar," which applies to Indians in Britain or for that matter in Canada, does not exist in any significant degree in the United States.[26] But once Indians become vocal in American affairs, especially in its polity, it is reasonable to assume that they will be targets of differentiation (if not discrimination) as much as any other group in the United States. For, in America, the life chances of members of an ethnic group always revolve around politics. Those who eschew politics will remain forever marginals on the American scene.

Ths emergence of Indian ethnic enclaves in various parts of the United States is a recent phenomenon, not more than two decades old. During this period, hundreds of Indian organisations and scores of Indian ethnic newspapers have sprung up throughout the country. Social mixing among Indians, no matter of what subcultural or regional background in India, is quite common. This has laid the ground-work for the Indian ethnic community. It remains to be seen if this community will have a political impact on the United States or on India in any significant degree.

FOOT NOTES

1. Harold R. Isaacs, *Images of Asia*, New York : Capricorn Books, 1962 (published originally as *Scratches on Our Minds*, 1958), p. 283.
2. *ibid.*
3. The estimate of the Indian population in the United States comes

from various sources, including reports of the United States Immigration and Naturalisation Service and the data available from various studies of Indians in the United States.

4. *Literary Digest*, March 10, 1923, and Harold R. Isaacs, *op. cit.*, p, 284.
5. Harold R. Isaacs, *ibid.*, p. 285.
6. For the British situation, see among others, Michael H. Lyon, "Ethinicity in Britain : the Gujarati Tradition," in *New Community*, Vol. 2, No. 1, Winter 1972-3, pp. 1-11.
7. H.S. Morris, "Ethnic Groups" in David L. Sills (editor), *International Encyclopedia of the Social Sciences*, New York : The Macmillon Company & The Free Press, 1968, p. 167.
8. The world-wide ethnic situation is not comparable unless one states the purpose of classification. The Indian culture cannot be separated *per se* from the collective culture of the linguistic groups, *e.g.*, Bengalis, Hindi-speaking areas of Bihar, Uttar Pradesh and Rajsthan, Punjabis, Gujaratis, Marathis, Orissans, Andhras, Tamils, Karnatakas and Malayalis, etc. So, in terms of the definition chosen by us, these groups do not qualify as ethnic groups. In fact, there is no Indian culture different from the culture of these linguistic and regional groups, which form the Indian society. There are minorities in India, which are defined in the Indian constitution ; then there are subcultures as well.

   In the Soviet Union, there are 120 major ethnic groups of which Great Russians were only 53% in population in 1970, (vide. Richard M. Burkey, *Ethnic and Radical Groups*, Menlo Park, California : Cummings Publishing Company, 1978), p. 23. Compared to the Soviet Union, where the ethnic groups constitute 47% of the minority population, Chinese People's Republic (CPR) has only 45 million people in 54 minority enthnic groups, when the population of Han Chinese is over 900 million people, (vide. June Teufel Dreyer, "Ethnic Relations in China," in *The Annals of the American Academy of Political and Social Science*, Vol. 433, September 1977, p. 101). It should be borne in mind that the Russian and Chinese classifications are official and administrative categories although they meet the requirements of the sociological definition adopted by us.

   The Indian situation of ethnicity if we must adopt this word is more like the Chinese situation than the Russian one. In the United States, Protestants by self-identification comprise 55% of the

American population, which is an important reason for identifying American culture with WASP (White Anglo-Saxon Protestant) culture. See, Charles H. Anderson, *White Protestant Americans*, Englewood Cliffs, New Jersey : Prentice-Hall, Inc., 1970, p. 3. and Richard M. Burkey, *Ethnic and Radical Groups, passim.* Ethnicity in India may also show important similarities with enthnicity in the United States.

9. See, R.A. Schermerhorn, *Ethnic Plurality in India* Tuscon : The University of Arizona Press, 1978.
10. For a theoretical analysis of the caste system, see Baidya Nath Varma, "The Caste System of India," in Baidya Nath Varma (editor), *Contemporary India,* New York : Asia Publishing House, 1964, pp. 59-81.
11. Milton M. Gordon, *Assimilation in American Life*, New York : Oxford University Press, 1964.
12. J. Milton Yinger. "Ethnicity in Complex Societies: Structural, Cultural, and Characterological Factors," in Lewis A. Coser and Otto N. Larsen (editors), *The Uses of Controversy in Sociology,* New York : The Free Press, 1978, p. 200.
13. Through the efforts of some of the Indian community leaders in the United States, the Bureau of Census decided to count "Asian Indians" separately in the 1980 census,
14. The concept of "ethnic renaissance" has been used and elaborated in Baidya Nath Varma, *The Sociology and Politics of Development : A Theoretical Study* London : Routledge & Kegan Paul Ltd., (1980).
15. Rudyard Kipling was perhaps responsible for creating early stereotypes about India in the Western mind. The most famous quotation from Kipling is :

    Oh, East is East, and West is West, and
      never the twain shall meet,
    Till Earth and Sky stand presently at
      God's great Judgement Seat ;

    However, in order to have perspective on Kipling, one must add the missing lines which follow the quotation :

    But there is neither East nor West,
      Border, nor Breed, nor Birth,
    When two strong men stand face to face
      tho' they come from the ends of the earth !

    See, Rudyard Kipling, "The Ballad of East and West." in *The Works of Rudyard Kipling*, Roslyn, New York : Black's Readers Service, no date, pp. 53-55.

16. Harold R. Isaacs, *op. cit.*, p, 270.
17. *ibid.*, pp. 290-316.
18. *ibid.*, p. 324.
19. *ibid.*
20, Among others, see M.V. Kamath, *Tha United States and India 1776-1976*, Washinton, D.C. : The Embassy of India, 1976, especially chapter 4 ("In the Cause of Independence").

    The involvement of American ethnics in the affairs of the state to which they relate themselves in terms of their origins is nothing new. A large section of the American Jewry is involved in the affairs of Israel. So are the Blacks involved in Africa, especially South Africa, and the Irish enthnics interested in the future of Northern Ireland. The sociological implications of such involvements have, however, not adequately been spelled out so far in our judgement.
21. The Government of India helps in the effort by facilitating communication and aid given by the Indian organisations to any particular village it "adopts" for giving aid.
22. The Association of Indians in America is active in this field.
23. The author had the privilege of presiding over one such debate on "Should the People from the Indian Subcontinent Seek Protected Class Status ?", held in New York on March 26, 1977, sponsored by a number of Indian associations, in which American experts, such as Nathan Glazer, American administration representatives, and Indian experts presented the pros and cons of the matter. There seemed to be no consensus in this meeting.
24. This meeting was arranged by the Association of Indians in America.
25. In this connection, the Indian community was generally pleased that the department store, Bloomingdale's, reportedly spent nine million dollars (including 1 million on publicity) for selling Indian merchandise to the American buyers under the promotional title of "Fantasy India" in 1978.
26. The Canadian episodes of discrimination against Indians are vividly portrayed in the Indian ethnic press of the United States.

WHITHER THE ASIAN INDIAN FAMILY? : SOME GENERAL THEORETICAL NOTES

5

Whither the Asian Indian Family?: Some General Theoretical Notes

INTRODUCTION

I AM no expert on the Asian Indian family. However, the published studies I have seen, empirical and impressionistic, convince me that much research needs to be done on this topic. The following observations along theoretical lines are made to orient the researchers toward some significant problems. I hope that my observations will also have some value for individual guidance, especially when conflict or crisis occurs in the family.

I wish to indicate that I look at the Asian Indian family both in terms of its roots in the Indian civilisational values and its adjustment to the imperatives of the American society. My references to the published studies on the American family are meant to be of heuristic value in the study of the Asian Indian family.

In a real sense, empirical studies in the discipline of sociology began with the study of the institution of marriage and family in the United States. Such studies were meant to understand the strengths and weaknesses of the American family system and to predict the occurrence of divorces. However, although much is known today about the stability of the family, little help is available in predicting divorce rates. I wish to emphasise this point because many other institutional forms of behaviour can be predicted fairly accurately in American society but family behaviour remains an inscrutable phenomenon. This is not to suggest that well-documented studies of the ethnic families in the United States are not available. In fact, the perspective I will adopt in discussing the Asian Indian family is guided by many hypotheses availale in the studies of the American ethnic family systems.

It should be mentioned that although some scholars treat the linguistic and regional groups of India as ethnic, I do not do so. There is no India or Indian civilisation devoid of its regional population.[1] However, my clarification of this point for India does not affect our analysis here because all the Asian Indians are considered one ethnic group by the American population, and the Indian immigrants from various regions also behave as one ethnic group in the United States.

THE ASIAN INDIAN HERITAGE

The Asian Indian family will be examined now in terms of its Indian roots. The problems of acculturation and adjustment of the first generation of Indians in the United States will be taken up first. The questions of the autonomy of the nuclear family and conflicts within it will be explored as far as possible. Then, the development and growth of the Asian Indian family in the United States will be highlighted The role of the second generation of the Asian Indian family will be briefly discussed in the perspectives of the socialisation of the child and the autonomous growth of the Asian Indian family in America.

In my earlier writings, I have called the year 1968 as the "line of the great divide" by which I mean that the Indians who immigrated to the United States before 1968 but after World War II had a different footing and somewhat different expectations of America than those who came after that year.[2] The small population of the Asian Indians settled on the West Coast in California are not included in this categorisation because their orientations when they came at the turn of the century were quite different from those of the students and the professionals who came to the United States after the Second World War. The post-1968 generation had better mutual support and assistance from friends and relatives who were already in the United States than the earlier generation of Post World War II immigrants. Although the sense of security was higher in the post-1968 generation, the incidence of conflicts was no less mitigated because of the nature of competition and the pressure of social mobility in the American society.

We will now examine the case of a hypothetical person X in studying the problems of acculturation, autonomy and growth of the Asian Indian family. Let us assume that X is a male, which is true in the majority of cases of the first generation immigrants to the United States. However, in the case of India it seems that X faces less trauma than most immigrants from other nations. X is either from a village, a small town, or a metropolis in India but in all these cases, he is more educated, upwardly mobile and anticipates constant change in his life unlike the past immigrants from other nations. He is psychologically prepared to face any crisis developing in his career or life goals. Once he is in the United States, and after getting started in his job, he feels the need for emotional support. This is met from friends and family, if any, within commuting distance from where he lives. Occasionally dating takes place but that is only for satisfying the need for new experience. His friends are more likely to be Indians than Americans in the beginning.

Ties to India get reaffirmed through correspondence with other friends and family members in India. This has been the common pattern of all other immigrants to the United States. The exception in the case of India, especially with regard to the post-1968 immigrants, is the fact of visits to India every two years or so, which has incidentally also kept Air India very solvent when other airlines have been going through a period of crisis in recent years. The remittances of the Asian Indians to their families in India not only maintain strong bonds between generations living across the seven seas, as the Indian saying goes, but also have helped the government of India recently in managing well its problem of balance of payments.

Once X gets fairly settled in his job in the United States, in most cases he goes back to India to get married and bring his wife to the United States. Of course, if he was already married before coming to the United States, there is no question of a new marriage. He brings his wife and children, if any, to live with him in the United States. These marriages are predominantly "arranged" as is customary in India. Even in the case X takes recourse to matrimonial advertisements in an Indian newspaper or American ethnic journal catering to Asian Indians, the strength and weaknesses of his marital bond are not very different from arranged marriages.

When marital choice of partners is made by parents or relatives in India, they make sure of the compatibility of the persons to be joined in matrimony. In the case of marriage through newspaper advertisements, the partners have no more information about one another than that provided by go-between persons who "arrange" marriages. The question of love is a new quotient in the life of the Asian Indian immigrant.

I find that love has at least couple of dozen different meanings in the sociological literature.[3] After looking at them carefully, I have come to the conclusion that love can have equal chance of starting either before or after marriage with a person. In fact, Vera and David Mace, after examining marriages around the world, have come to the conclusion that the arranged marriage system of India is one of the most successful forms of marriage.[4] I wish to add my opinion that arranged marriages, in most cases, do develop as deep a bond and love between partners as the "romantic love complex" emphasised in the United States.

FAMILY ACCULTURATION

X is now living with his wife as a married couple in the United States. Either X is supporting his wife or they are both working. At home, life is full of freedoms and restrictions. No in-laws or extended family members are there to hamper one's desires and activities, but also no servants or cooks to do the family chores. Both partners learn to arrange their home life as they wish, perhaps the male seeking more of his male prerogatives as in India and the female asking for the cooperation and assistance of the husband in housework and child upbringing as the modern American values emphasise. The visits with other Indian families on weekends are a must which bolster the same values. Indian movies seen on home video sets are an important form of recreation. It is, however, in the temples and the mosques they go to pray, where traditional Indian civilisational values get reinforced all the time.

There is much verbal and written controversy over the role of the Indian female in the family life of India. Some claim that the woman is inferior to the man. Unfortunately, this issue has not been settled even by the anthropologists working in the field in India. The women's liberation movement is a new phenomenon in India.

Civilisational Values

I look at the role of the Indian woman in the Indian civilisational context as follows :[5]

As a *patni* (wife) to her *pati* (husband), she is *ardhāngini*—the other half of the body. Indian civilisation emphasises the following virtues in a woman :

Chastity—example, Sita

Dignity–example, Savitri

Purity—example, Ganga

Energy—example, Tara

Victory—example, Durga

In the Western civilisation today, the woman is thought of as a partner, who has rights, who is a worker and who has personal worth, commensurate with her earning capacity.

The civilisational life of India is depicted manifestly in the Ramayana and the Mahabharat, which are the epics eulogised by the folk as well as the urban people of India. Rama is the ideal king, husband, and brother. Sita is the ideal wife and the pride of womanhood. Lakshaman, Bharat and Shatrughna are ideal brothes. In the Ramayana, these roles are idealised to their heights. But in the Mahabharat they are cut down to size through the interplay of selfishness and conflict which are endemic to human life. If the Pandava brothers in Mahabharat are as devoted to each other as Rama and his brothers are in Ramayana, the Kaurava brothers do not demur in showing the hatred of stepbrotherliness toward the Pandavas in the Mahabharat. There is plenty in the story of these two epics to enlighten and guide the behaviour of an average Indian.

The hero of the Mahabharat is Krishna. Krishna Lila (Krishna's worldly round of activities) emphasises love. It is played as a dance drama in all parts of India. Krishna is *sānsārik*—worldly. Krishna plays various roles : Balkrishna (child), Gopi Krishna (lover to the Gopis), Radha Krishna (partner of Radha), Arjun Krishna (teacher of Arjun), and Dwaraka Krishna (king of Dwaraka).

Role Models

Ramayana's hero is Rama. Rama is *maryādā purushottum*-prestige personified. Unlike the Ramayana, the Mahabharat has many heroes. Between these two epics, there are role models available for every man and woman in India. Needless to say, one or another of these role models will be subconsciously or sometimes consciously adopted by X and his wife in the pursuit of a happy life even in the United States. When they have children of their own, the role models will have great significance, especially in times of distress or confiict. This is the civilisational context of the Asian Indian family.

The post-1968 generation of Asian Indians has seen the emergence of hundreds of Indians organisations in the United States. This was not true earlier. Many of these organisations are regional, but some are national in scope. The battle for leadership which seems to be ingrained in the Indian character, has come to the forefront and new role models, especially of leadership, are being sought. Perhaps five such role models of the twentieth century may be mentioned here. These are : Mahatma Gandhi, Jawaharlal Nehru, Bal Gangadhar Tilak, Jayaprakash Narayan, and B.R. Ambedkar. The first two of these five leaders were consensus-seeking and evolutionary in their approach. The next three were uncompromising and revolutionary in demeanour. Indira Gandhi may perhaps be mentioned as the sixth role model not only for women, but for all who seek power as well as conciliation among divergent and even opposite points of view.

The familial life of X and his professional life are enriched by the knowledge of the Indian civilisational values and the twentieth century cultural context of India's modernisation. X can argue, debate, defend, and enhance his position in his family, among his friends, neighbours, and professional colleagues with full faith in the virtues of his own civilisation. His wife can repeat the same with equal success. His growing children will learn the strengths and weaknesses of their parents by participating in the real life drama that unfolds itself in the Asian Indian family in its American milieu. It is indeed a very fascinating drama.

FAMILY AUTONOMY

I believe that family autonomy is an important concept in trying to understand the functioning of the family in the United States The norms of the American family are that the family should be monogamous, nuclear, neolocal, bilateral, and democratic in nature. Monogamy itself is a legal requirement. The rest of the institutional structure is also common to all families although in reality there may be a range of divergences from these norms. A nuclear family is the one where husband, wife, and unmarried children live together. However, at present not more than 32% of the American families are nuclear in the above sense.[6] Neolocality implies that the married couple should live separately from the parents of either partner. Again, about one tenth of the married couples are not able to establish separate residence for at least one year for financial and other reasons.[7] Bilaterality involves common allegiance of both partners to at least two generations of ancestors of both the groom and the bride. Democracy conveys the idea that decisions in the family should be made together by the husband and the wife in consultation with their children.

America has been called the melting pot and the above structural form of the American family emphasises the norm that ethnic groups should give up the ancestral customs of their home countries and accept the American norms totally. In reality, however, some ethnic groups have maintained their ancestral customs for a long time despite their residence in the United States. The Jews, the Italian Americans, the Hispanics, the Chinese Americans, among others, are good examples of such cases.[8] But, as the second generation of American born children arrives, the predominant American norms seem to apply even to these ethnic groups.[9]

The most famous American study of acculturation is *The Polish Peasant in Europe and America*, by W.I. Thomas and Florian Znaniecki, published in the 1920's in five volumes.[10] It has also been called "the first Bible of empirical sociology" in the United States. What happend to the Poles in their migration from Poland and settlement in the United States tells a fascinating story which applies to all later immigrants equally well. The acculturation of the Italian American has been studied in detail, especially in regard to the changes in attitudes from the first to the second generation.[11] These studies provide numerous hypotheses for testing on the Asian Indian family. We will incorporate them in depicting the *autonomy* and *growth* of the Asian Indian family.

One more theoretical note. I believe that just as the American society emphasises autonomy for the individual so also it demands the same type of autonomy for nuclear families. Individual social mobility is the reigning norm of America, which also creates anxieties and conflicts in the lives and goals of individuals. For the Asian Indian the autonomous development of the family often creates disharmony within the family and conflict between the nuclear family and the extended kin. Such conflicts, however, can also help in cementing the bond as has been pointed out by Georg Simmel in his essays on conflict.[12] But they often can lead to disruption and even the disintegration of the nuclear family through separation and divorce. One must look carefully at the American environment and its pressures on the family in formulating hypotheses about the growth of the Asian Indian family.

INTERMARRIAGE

If X marries another Indian in India, it is more likely to be a person from the same caste. However, sometimes, intercaste if not interregional marriage, also takes place. If X marries someone in the United States, it is more likely to be an intermarriage. The same would be true if he married an Indian from another country or an American in the United States. Such marrgiages are usually based on love and are not very different from the pattern followed in the United States. In the case of intermarriage, the life of the Asian Indian family begins with greater autonomy than arranged marriage or India-based marriage. However, there is strain on the part of the husband if he wants his wife to be accepted by his parents in India. In such cases, a visit to India by the couple has the highest priority on the list of family obligations.

Family autonomy takes many forms. For instance, the life of a married couple in the United States demands an adherence to their professional responsibilities first, which mean incorporating some of their American colleagues in their circle of friendships. However, by and large, the Indian friends take priority in terms of frequency of visits and mutual sharing of joys and sorrows. The orientation to the kin of the American partner has also some satisfaction.

Intermarriages in the United States do involve some dating on the part of the first generation immigrant from India. In the second generation, the opportunity for dating increases. It should be noted that dating does not create the complication in the family of intermarried couples as it does in the families where both parents come from the same caste in India. The autonomy of the family of intermarried couples paves the way for the children to meet the American norms of courtship, love and marriage, which is not the case for the majority of the Asian Indian families.

CHILD REARING

The Asian Indian family treats its firstborn infant in the United States the same way as the Americans do. The girls have pink attires and the boys have blue ones. Their cribs and the baby carriages are likely to be more sophisticated and expensive than the average American infant has. It shows the income status of the Asian Indian family as well as a subconscious desire to show off to one's friends and neighbours one's status and marital strength.

Up to the age of four, the upbringing of the child is very smooth with little conflict within the family. The Asian Indian family also follows the American pattern of having two or three children within the first five years of marriage. As the family grows, the chores increase and the Indian husband learns quickly to adjust to being a role partner to his wife in taking care of the daily necessities of the children. It is during the childhood stages from ages four to thirteen that the civilisational standards start to be applied to their behaviour more by the mother than by the father. During teenage years of the children, the maximum amount of intergenerational conflict shows up within the Asian Indian family as it does in the American family.

The disco music and dance and sports for the youth are as much favourite pastimes of the second generation of Asian Indians as they are of their American counterparts. The parents allow them these privilieges either in the basement of their houses or in discotheques and sports fields If the parents participate at all in their activities, it is the father who goes with the boys to the ball games and other sports events. The mother remains aloof, perhaps watching from a distance how her male children are growing up. Some families provide opportunity for learning Indian classical dances, especially for girls. The Indian woman imparts the virtues of Indian womanhood to her daughter and encourages her husband similarly to instil Indian values in the sons.

The Indian woman, in my judgement, is the carrier of the Indian civilisation *par excellence,* and the Indian man merely supports what his wife does in the inculcation of these values. The husband's attention is more directed to guiding his children in their career decisions rather than in their day to day activities. Religious festivals and feasts reinforce Indian civilisational values for all.

TEENAGE DEVELOPMENT

Teenage is one of the most convulsive periods of socialisation in the American family. In fact, by looking at the traumas of the American teenager, G. Stanley Hall, an American psychologist, had advanced the theory of "adolescent upheaval" for the development of personality.[13] He claimed that adolescent upheaval was a universal phenomenon. However, Margaret Mead, an anthropologist, in her book, *Coming of Age in Samoa,* disproved this theory by showing the smoothness of transition to adulthood in Samoan culture.[14] Without going into a discussion of the merits and weaknesses of these theories, I would like to state that adolescent upheaval is a fact of American society created by the needs of the overarching value of individual success in America and the guidance of much of people's leisure time activities by the messages conveyed through the mass media.

America demands progress and it defines progress in terms of change. First, there was a call for progress, or change for the better. But now it seems that change for its own sake has bacome the norm of American society. No one can resist changes occurring in fads and fashions in clothing, beauty aids and sports, but when vital institutions of society, especially its core institution, the family, are affected by the whims of the manipulators of the American mass media, something has to give. And if this something happens to be a set of coveted values of the family system, then, hell breaks loose.

Let us take a couple of examples. Up until the publication of the Kinsey reports on *Sexual Behavior in the Human Male* (1948) and *Sexual Behavior in the Human Female* (1953),[15] premarital chastity was a valued norm preached equally by the church and the public leaders. Of course, what Kinsey and his associates did was merely to explore the human frailties and sexual practices of the *American male* and the *American female.* The first book raised a national hue and cry, and the press and the pulpit denounced such studies of sex as immoral.[16] But the tide of change that swept over American in the 1950's and 1960's transformed even the attitude of the Church towards sex and premarital chastity.[17]

Another related issue concerns pornography. It is one of the most legally involved and hotly debated social issues in America, and yet the guardians of morality in American society would not permit it to be examined before the light of reason.

The earliest books on eroticism come from India where even some of the temples carry sculptural engravings of erotic art.[18] India does not face the psychological problems of sexual denial which an average American is made to feel through the crosscutting messages of sexual revolution and sexual abnormality. Unfortunately, the teenage children of America are the direct victims of the barrage of contradictory messages coming from the mass media and society's gatekeepers.

Let us consider a second issue. In the 1950's, the median

age for women at first marriage was about twenty years in the United States.[19] It meant that at the time of first marriage either they were teenagers or they had just passed their teens. After their marriage it was discovered that they were not seeking parental guidance for the bearing and rearing of their children. Instead, they took the advice of their age mates and other married couples in making decisions on these matters. Occasionally, the pediatrician was considered the best authority on how to bring up a child. In fact, in the 1930's there was a rebellion against punishing the child no matter how much it misbehaved because it was felt that punishment would inhibit the child and obstruct the natural growth of its personality. This movement was called Rabelianism after a certain pediatrician named Dr. Rabel. This movement lost its weight in a couple of decades. The pediatricians in many instances were guided by some fuzzy-minded theorists who had instant answers to some of the most complex problems of life, such as the healthy growth of a newborn child. Such fads and fashions have unfortunately existed in many areas of family behaviour in the United States.

The Asian Indian teenage boys and girls face somewhat similar problems with regard to attitudes towards sex as the Americans do today. The American society, especially through the mass media, clothing and ornaments, leisure time pursuits and its dating complex, encourages a degree of freedom for boys and girls which the family or the church is not ready to accept and this creates conflict within the family. The girls are further vulnerable to pregnancy which enhances the volatility of the situation. The chaperoning of Hispanic families from Latin America is a cushion for the girl but the Asian family has little choice available in the matter. Either the teenagers should be permitted to date or they should not. This creates the maximum possibility of conflict between parents and children in the Asian Indian family. By the time the children are teenagers, the Asian Indian family has become fully autonomous, so that guidance or help from extended family o:

kin is neither sought nor is considered desirable. If at this point the family can make a democratic decision in which the parents permit the children to participate that will perhaps make for a healthier growth of the Asian Indian family.

OLD AGE

We do not know how many Asian Indian families we are considering here have parents who have retired from active professional life. But some families have brought their retired parents from India to live with them in the United States. This has created a problem both for the first generation Asian Indian immigrants and their retired parents coming to live with them. The parental bond of India is very much alive in the minds of all members of the family; the civilisational values are deep rooted.

The Sanskrit word for son is *putra*, whose derivation is *pum nām narakāt trāyate iti putrah*—a son is the one who rescues a person from the hell named *pum*. Given such a scriptural sanction and the love of Rama for his father King Dasaratha for whom he renounced his throne and went to the forest for fourteen years to keep the honour of his father, how could an Indian forsake his father in old age ? Moreover, the retired parents are in the stage of *vānaprashtha* (renunciation of familial obligations), one of the four stages of the Hindu *Varnāshrama Dharma*. Thus their presence in the family is not supposed to disturb the family habits and routine.

The grandparents have a habit of becoming unduly attached to the grandchildren in the United States as they do in India. This creates problems for the disciplining of the child in the Asian Indian family. The matter is further complicated by fact that the Asian Indian immigrants feel an obligation to visit only those friends on weekends where they could take their retired parents with them. The grandparents, on the other hand, have no other age group companions of their own with whom to talk. Their only consolation is to be with their son or daughter who are adults, and grandchildren, whose daily routine of life is very busy. The greatest pleasure of the grandparents comes in visiting the temples and ceremonial performances of the Asian Indian community.

The grandparents have not taken any active role in the affairs of the Asian Indian organisations. At the moment, it seems that either because of the paucity of their numbers or of their lack of motivation to be acculturated in the American society, many persons in the grandparents' role are half happy and half sad—happy to be in the company of their progenies and sad for being away from home, India, where they left behind all their other kin, all other joys and sorrows.

CONCLUSION

The Asian Indian family is in a dilemma. The dilemma is whether to conform to the norms of the average American family (which means urban middle class family) or to follow its Indian civilisational roots. The Asian Indian immigrant has come at the highest ladder of American society unlike his Western European predecessor. He has started high in the professions of the United States with a full willingness to absorb the American culture, but he cannot forget his ancient civilisational roots. The values inculcated in his childhood are the values of Rama and Krishna, Gandhi and Nehru, Patel and Jayaprakash, Ambedkar and a host of other Indian giants. The sacrifices of these heroes stand up in the memories of the Asian Indian immigrant.

The Asian Indian is a born philosopher. He comes to the United States full of hopes of success in his life. These hopes generally materialise for him but the fruits must be shared with family and kin. The family he creates in America is autonomous and full of responsibilities and obligations. The responsibilities are for one's wife or husband and children. Some other obligations are to the norms of extended family in India· If the divergences and contradictions between the norms of the family system in India and the American family system could be handled judiciously, it would be a healthy Asian Indian family. If the nuclear family of the Asian Indian breaks up under the strains of overambition or underachievement, it would not be the fault of the person's upbringing in India. The stresses and strains of America are too great to handle for anyone whose civilisational roots provide no guidance in such matters. Fortunately, for those who believe in tradition, the Mahabharat gives a full range of psychic conflicts and their resolutions, just as the Ramayana epitomises the monolithic roles of the ideal male in Rama and the ideal female in Sita.

America is a land of dreams. The Asian Indian immigrants are a band of dreamers. They want to scale the heights of the Himalayas. They want to measure the depths of the oceans. If the Indian civilisational values arise from the heights of Mount Kailash, the Ameriean system of modernity and progress provides the yardstick in terms of which the Asian Indian family's accomplishments can be measured. India and America, despite their global distance from one another, can come together through the Asian Indian. The Asian Indian family has to survive its initial trials in the United States. It has to accommodate both tradition and change. Only time can tell if the Asian Indian family will be lost in the American melting pot or will survive as an important ethnic group enriching the heritage of America and perpetuating its links with India.

FOOTNOTES

1. Baidya Nath Varma, "Indians As New Ethnics: A Theoretical Note," in Parmatma Saran and Edwin Eames (eds.), *The New Ethnics: Asian Indians in the United States* (New York: Praeger, 1980), pp. 30-32.
2. Baidya Nath Varma, "The Problems of Migration: The Asian

Indians in the United States," Paper presented at the Columbia University Faculty Seminar on Cultural Pluralism, 1982.

3. Some of the attributes of love in the published literature are : infatuation, sexual desire, to excite and satisfy one's sexual passion, sweeping experience, novelty, to be intimate, to share, tenderness, altruistic experience, compassion, satisfaction, enduring relationship.

   It is clear that the experience of love ranges from sexual satisfaction to altruism but the key seems to be mutuality and enduring relationship.

4. Vera Mace and David Mace, *How To Have A Happy Marriagc* (Nashville, Tennessee : Abingdon, 1983).
5. Baidya Nath Varma, "Indian Civilization : Some Unanswered Questions," Paper presented at Columbia University Faculty Seminar on Studies in Contemporary India, 1983.
6. "The American Family : Bent—Not Broken," *U.S. News and World Report*, June 16, 1980.
7. Robert F. Winch, *The Modern Family* (New York : Holt, Rinehart and Winston, 1971).
8. *Ibid.*
9. *Ibid.*
10. W.I. Thomas and Florian Znaniecki, *The Polish Peasant in Europe and America*, 5 vols. (Boston : Richard G. Badger, 1918-20).
11. Paul J. Campisi, "Ethnic Family Patterns : The Italian Family in the United States," *The American Journal of Sociology* (1948) : 443-449.
12. Georg Simmel. *Confiict and The Web of Group Affiliations* (Glencoe, Illinois : The Free Press, 1955).
13. G. Stanley Hall, *Adolescence* (New York : D. Appleton, 1904).

    See also Hans Gerth and C. Wright Mills, *Character and Social Structure* (New York : Harcourt, Brace and Company, 1953), pp. 141-147.
14. Margaret Mead, *Coming of Age in Samoa* (New York : Morrow, 1928.
15. Alfred C. Kinsey, Wardell Pomeroy, and Clyde Martin. *Sexual Behavior in the Human Male* (Philadelphia : Saunders, 1948). Alfred C. Kinsey and Paul Gebhard, *Sexual Behavior in the Human Female* (Philadelphia : Saunders, 1953).

16. See the various press reports at the time.

17. Rustom and Della Roy, *Honest Sex : A revolutionary sex ethic by and for concerned Christians* (New York : The New American Library, 1968).

18. *Kamasutra of Vatsyayana*, translated by S.C. Upadhyaya (Bombay : Taraporevala's Treasure House of Books, 1961). See also Kanwar Lal, *Immortal Khajuraho* (Delhi : Asia Press, 1965).

19. Ira L. Reiss, *Family System in America* (New York : Holt, Rinehart and Winston, 1980), p. 223.

Index